HOW TO WIN

THE **TOASTMASTERS**

WORLD CHAMPIONSHIP

of Public Speaking

2012 International Speech Contest

Jeremey Donovan

How to Win the Toastmasters World Championship of Public Speaking: 2012 International Speech Contest
Jeremey Donovan

Published in the United States by CreateSpace
ISBN: 1483931315
ISBN-13: 9781483931319
Library of Congress Control Number: 2013905987
CreateSpace Independent Publishing Platform
North Charleston, South Carolina

Hi David,

Thanks again for allowing me your permission to reprint the transcript of your World Championship speech in my next book.

Enclosed, please find a copy of my new 3rd book which covers the 2012 contest.

I'd be indebted for an objective review on Amazon.

About the Author

The journey is the reward.

Lao Tzu, *Tao Te Ching*

Jeremey Donovan joined Toastmasters in 1998 following a job change that prevented him from remaining an introvert. He earned his Distinguished Toastmaster accreditation in 2012. Jeremey is the author of three books, including *How to Deliver a TED Talk,* the number one Amazon best seller in public speaking. He is also group vice-president of marketing at Gartner Inc., the world's leading information technology research and advisory company with $1.6 billion in annual revenue.

Contents

Preface

Each year, thirty thousand of Toastmaster's 280,000 members compete to determine who will be crowned the World Champion of Public Speaking. The winners are transformed instantly from unknowns to royalty—mobbed at conferences by well-wishers and sought after as sages by legions of speakers dreaming of replicating the victors' success.

Some champions, like Craig Valentine, Darren LaCroix, and David Brooks, become highly successful motivational speakers and trainers. Others, like David Henderson and Mark Brown, go back to their day jobs forever transformed by their experience.

On an early Saturday morning in August 2012, nine of the best speakers in the world sat, stood, or paced backstage at the Hilton Orlando Bonnet Creek Convention Center. For most of them, the crowd of 1,500 fellow Toastmasters would be the largest audience they had ever and would ever address. Having won their respective semifinal rounds two days before, these nine had one simple task—to deliver the speech of their life in just five to seven minutes.

As with most high-stakes competitions, this one had a catch. The contestants had polished and delivered the same speech, their best speech, through the club, area, division, district, and semifinal rounds spanning six months. However, in the finals, each of the nine speakers was required to deliver a completely new speech. While it was safe to assume that every speaker at this level had long since developed the speech he or she would use in the final round, one cannot overestimate how difficult it was to mentally reboot and stay focused with just a day and a half between the semifinal and the final round. The contestants had to take their second-best content out of their back pocket, dust it off, and polish it enough to be their new best speech.

In the chapters that follow, I will deconstruct the speeches of prior World Champions alongside the nine speeches of the 2012 Toastmasters World Championship finalists including (in speaking order): Andrew Kneebone, Stuart Pink, Ronald E. Melvin, Brian Corey, Diane Parker, Palaniappa Subramaniam, Kenny Ray Morgan, Ryan Avery, and Mario Lewis. Each of these speakers stood on the shoulders of giants, leveraging the best practices of prior winners while adding their unique voice and style.

The approach that I took to uncover the secrets of these nine master storytellers and their predecessors is both a blessing and a curse. Tread wisely by heeding the advice that 1995 Toastmasters World Champion Mark Brown gave me:

Some people get the DVD set of past winners and deconstruct every speech. They count how many steps people take before they say a word and what color suit to wear if you are speaker number six versus speaker number three. I did not do any of that. There is a danger in over-polishing your speech. If you go too far, you will lose your sense of frankness and genuineness. Bring yourself, your experience, your voice, your life, and your message to the forefront. Strive to leave the audience with something of value and the rest will come.

Author's Note: In adherence to the "fair use" rule of the US copyright law, this book makes limited use of copyrighted excerpts from the Toastmasters World Championship of Public Speaking for the purpose of criticism and commentary, and for the purpose of providing a public good by elevating the presentation skills of aspiring speakers. It is my hope that this book significantly increases the number of people exposed to the organization and its mission. All company and product names mentioned herein are the trademarks or registered trademarks of their respective owners.

CHAPTER 1:
Taking the Stage

Tip #1: Craft a memorable title that triggers insatiable curiosity

After reading the contest rules and confirming that the timers and judges were ready, contest master George Yen kicked off the 2012 Toastmasters World Championship of Public Speaking: "Our first contestant is Andrew Kneebone. The Story of Two Kneebones. The Story of Two Kneebones. Andrew Kneebone."

A speaker's ability to engage the audience begins before he or she even steps onto the stage. Upon hearing the speech title, each audience member's brain kicks into high gear trying to figure out what is coming next. Strive to trigger curiosity to find out both "Why" and "How" with your speech title. Speech titles that prompt "Who?" "What?" and "Where?" are generally less potent.

The most powerful open-ended question to incite in a speech is "Why?" Even if people have paid to listen to you speak, they have an invisible shield up until you give them a reason to believe. Prompting the audience to ask "Why" draws out the elephant in the room so that you can satisfy it right at the beginning of your speech. The second most powerful open-ended question that you want to prompt in a motivational speech is "How?" For instance, if your talk is about happiness, then setting up a burning desire in your audience to know "How" signals that you will fulfill a promise to deliver your magic recipe for blissful living.

When you hear "The Story of Two Kneebones," what questions arise in your mind? The first is passing curiosity about where the speaker will take his play on words. Perhaps he will use 'knees' in some sort of too-clever metaphor, as is typical in Toastmasters speeches. Or, perhaps he will talk about two people that share his last name. In this case, Andrew chose the latter and told a story about his persistent father and an intrepid nineteenth century ancestor.

The second question is simply, "What is the story?" The problem with this title is that it prompts neither a "Why" nor a "How" question. If the audience members are not turned off by the too-cute metaphor, then they will be satisfied completely once they have heard the story. At best, this title sets the audience up to be entertained; it does not set them up to be inspired.

To see what a great title looks like, you merely need to glance back at the past twenty-six years of winning speeches. In descending order of impact, here are the types of titles that have been used: maxims, imperatives, verb phrases, adjective phrases, exclamations, noun phrases, and sentences.

Maxims are powerful because they simultaneously deliver the core message of the speech while prompting 'how', 'why', and often other questions. Examples of maxims include Jim Key's "Never Too Late" in 2003, Otis Williams Jr.'s "It's Possible" in

1993, Don Johnson's "A Many-Splendored Thing" in 1989, and Harold Patterson's "The Pain Passes" in 1987.

Imperatives typically have the same potent effect as maxims. You can see why immediately with LaShunda Rundles' "Speak!" from 2008, David Nottage's "Get Up" from 1996, and Dana LaMon's "Take a Chance" from 1992. Jerry Starke's "Please Don't Walk On Mother's Roses" from 1988 is far more subtle, and therefore far more memorable.

A close third in terms of impact are verb phrases. Edward Hearn's 2006 "Bouncing Back" prompts "Why?" "How?" and "Who?" The same holds true for Morgan McArthur's 1994 "Stuck to a Bucket." McArthur's title has that same subtle yet memorable quality that Jerry Starke's title had.

Adjective phrases and exclamations are rare. In fact, there has only been one of each in the past twenty-six years. Jock Elliot's adjective title "Just So Lucky" in 2011 described a positive state of being. Darren LaCroix's exclamation "OUCH!" in 2001 took the opposite approach in describing a state of pain. In both cases, the titles were inextricably linked to the content of the speeches. Jock Elliot shared how he was just so lucky to have the friends of his blood, the friends of his times, and the friends of his heart. Darren LaCroix used the pain of physically falling down as a metaphor for having the resilience to persevere in the face of failure, doubt, and rejection.

Though not the most stimulating, nouns and noun phrases are the most common titles used in winning Toastmasters speeches.

Noun-based titles are less powerful since the first question they typically prompt is, "What?" Intangible nouns make for more thought-provoking titles as compared with tangible nouns. This is highlighted in the following group of winning titles based on intangible concepts: Vikas Jhingran's "The Swami's Question" from 2007, Lance Miller's "The Ultimate Question" from 2005, Randy Harvey's "Lesson's From Fat Dad" from 2004, Dwayne Smith's "Music in the Key of Life" from 2002, Craig Valentine's "The Key to Fulfillment" from 1999, and Mark Brown's "A Second Chance" from 1995.

Next, consider the group of tangible noun titles that spotlight people, places, and things. Andrew Kneebone's choice of people mirrored David Henderson's "The Aviators" from 2010. Brett Rutledge suggested a location with "My Little World" in 1998. Rounding out the list of tangibles are thing-based titles including: Mark Hunter's "A Sink Full of Green Tomatoes" from 2009, Ed Tate's "One of Those Days" from 2000, Willie Jones' "A Warm Boot" from 1997, and David Brooks' "Silver Bullets" from 1990.

Full sentences make very unusual speech titles. Since they are by definition closed-ended, they put the speaker at an immediate disadvantage. That is not to say that you cannot win with a speech that is a sentence; it is just going to be that much more challenging. Two speeches with titles in this category have won, but both are from quite a while back. They are David Ross' "The Train's Still Rollin'" from 1991 and Arabella Bengson's "We Can Be Pygmalion" from 1986.

The common trait of the winning titles is they prime you beforehand by inciting curiosity and then persist afterward by being sensory. In addition, to be memorable, your title needs to stand out from the titles of all the other speeches in your contest. Since most speakers choose nouns, why not zig when they zag by choosing something more exotic.

Tip #2: Make your title as short as possible

Conciseness stands out as the one quality above all else that makes a speech title memorable. Let's take another look at "The Story of Two Kneebones." One of the unwritten rules of speechcraft is to never announce that you are going to tell a story. (The same rule applies to telling jokes.) Just tell it. The title "Two Kneebones" would have been better, not great, but better.

Over the past twenty-six years, winning speeches averaged just three words when rounding to the nearest whole number. Two titles—"Speak!" and "OUCH!"—used only one word to do the job. Six words was the maximum.

You might be tempted to stand out with a very long speech title. Though not a contest winner, the most viewed Toastmasters speech on YouTube as of this writing is Andy Dooley's excellent 2006 speech entitled "A short but unbelievably intriguing tale of how destiny unexpectedly showed her true colors against the backdrop of pure white snow on a Colorado mountaintop while all other conditions remained normal." At thirty-one words, this title breaks the bank! Just after the contest master said "pure white snow" the audience erupted into rolling laughter that continued for the duration. This approach is certainly fine for a one-off speech in any environment. Moreover, it can help you win in the International Speech Contest up through and including the District level. But, it is likely to fail after that on the basis of being memorable for its shock value rather than for its message. Judges at the highest levels are critical of tricks that are little more than attention grabbers. Perhaps proving the point, Mr. Dooley gave the speech a new and improved title—"My Date With Destiny"—when he uploaded his video for the world to see.

Titles are of course just one facet of speech construction. A bad speech with a great title will not win. And, a great speech with a terrible title can win. But, why not stack the odds in your favor by crafting a great speech title?

Tip #3: Speaking order does not matter, your speech matters

Andrew Kneebone is about as well-rounded as they come. A modern renaissance man, he combines the right-brain talents of photography and speaking with the left-brain talents of engineering and project management. He is the kind of guy that you imagine was a paperboy growing up—which is in fact exactly the case. Of his two-year stint, he proudly notes on his LinkedIn profile: "From 4:30 am - 6:00 am every day come rain, hail or shine, I would ride around the streets of Barooga delivering papers. For a total sum of $20 a week. Tungsten hard work ethic or complete and utter sucker?"

But despite his talents and intense drive, Andrew as the first speaker seemed to be at a massive disadvantage even before he took the stage. The conventional wisdom in speech contests is that no matter how effective your speech, you have little or no chance of winning if you are one of the first speakers in the draw. And worse, being chosen speaker number one is considered to be the curse of death. On some level that makes sense. After all, the judges have yet to calibrate what great looks like and your fellow contestants can adjust their delivery just enough to edge you out.

As a caveat, what I am about to do drives the past winners of the Toastmasters World Championship crazy; in my mind, I can conjure every one of them rolling his or her eyes at me for spending even an ounce of energy on speaking order. Still, everyone wonders, so it is a factor worth examining.

Over the twenty-six contests spanning 1987 to 2012, the average position of the winner was 5.6. With an average of 9.2 contestants (most years have nine finalists but there are some years with ten), you would expect the average position of the winner to be 4.6 if there were no speaking-order bias. The big question is whether 5.6 is statistically different from 4.6 given only twenty-six years of data. I will save you the pain of dusting off your college statistics textbook and just tell you that a statistician would tell Andrew not to worry. The average winning position of 5.6 is right on the boundary of unusual but still explainable as ordinary variation.

Another way to think about whether or not Andrew should have been worried is to look back at how often, if ever, the first speaker won the contest. In twenty-six years, if there were no speaking-order bias, you would expect the first speaker would have won somewhere between two and three times. Fortunately for Andrew, David Ross in 1991 and Dana LaMon in 1992 rose to the top of the podium despite their supposedly unlucky draw.

You can drive yourself crazy with statistics. For example, no fourth speaker has won in the past 26 years. Does that mean you should just give up if you draw the fourth straw? Of course not, that would be ridiculous. The fact of the matter is that there is no rigorous statistical proof that speaking order matters in the World Championship. Set your mind free. Speaking order does not belong in your mind—you have no control over it and it does not matter. The best speech will win.

Tip #4: Take the stage with confidence bridging the audience's energy to the tone of your content

As Andrew walked onto the stage, there were telltale signs that he was nervous. He took his first several steps with his head slightly down. He also looked down, albeit subtly, several more times before uttering his first words. His face alternated between a forced smile and intense concentration. Just before speaking, he closed his eyes, took a visibly deep breath, and loosened up his shoulders.

There is no shame in being nervous, especially with nearly 1,500 excited audience members expecting to hear one of the best speeches ever delivered. Public speaking induces anxiety no matter who you are (and anybody that tells you otherwise is flat-out lying). However, to win at the highest level of competition, you must mask your nervousness by channeling your energy into calm confidence. Even though the timer did not start until Andrew uttered his first word, he was being judged consciously or subconsciously from the moment he walked onto the stage. For better or worse, everything counts.

History shows that it is not impossible to recover from an unfavorable first impression. Ed Hearn, the 2006 World Champion, walked in with his head slightly down and even failed to shake the hand of the contest master. The year before that, the victorious Lance Miller combined looking down several times with nervously swaying his hands and his body.

For the most part, however, people who went on to win the World Championship held their head up, sported a consistently confident smile, and walked with a smooth pace. In most cases, your entrance should be remarkable neither for its timidity nor for its exuberance.

Your entrance should bridge the audience's energy to the tone of your content. In the Toastmasters International Speech

Contest, the tone is typically inspirational. However, if you are delivering a more somber message, then your pace of movement and your facial expressions should be far more subdued.

Even during the World Championship, speakers choose widely different degrees of entertainment. When the mix is weighted more heavily toward fun and frivolity, speakers should bring that context into how they take the stage. The 2009 World Champion, Mark Hunter, holds the title for highest-energy entrance. Confined to a wheelchair following a water skiing accident thirty years prior, Mr. Hunter rode out wearing a smile of sheer delight. His eyebrows were raised high, his high mouth was wide open, and his tongue even made an appearance. He set the tone very appropriately for a speech sprinkled with whimsical language and physicality that tied to the core message that love is what matters.

The Story of Two Kneebones

© 2012 Andrew Kneebone

http://www.ak-p.co

Central message(s)	Perseverance; Respect
Duration	6.98 minutes
Words per minute	108
Laughs per minute	0.86

Table 1.1: Vital statistics for *The Story of Two Kneebones* by Andrew Kneebone

(Introduction)

This story is about passion, obsession, and blood. Contest Chair, fellow Toastmasters and guests, allow me to introduce you to the two people I will be speaking about this morning.

The person on my right lived in England in the nineteenth century and sailed from Cornwall to Melbourne, Australia when he heard there was gold to be found. He was so successful he brought his four brothers out from England and bought them all farms. He wrote his life story down in a journal, with a twist. It was a poem, one long poem, from start to finish. And this from a man who never went to school.

The person on my left heard about this man's story, and heard that they shared the same last name. Introducing Henry Kneebone and Stuart Kneebone, my father.

When my father learned of Henry's journal, this started a passion which became an obsession to find and read that journal. And this journey went across two decades; and I was fortunate enough to witness this four times.

(Part One)

"Andrew? What are you doing?"

"Nothing."

"Well, stop it, and come here. It's about time you learned Henry Kneebone."

With that, he gave me a small piece of paper. "This is his life story."

"It's a little small, dad."

"It's not his whole life story, it's just a piece, but I will find the rest."

(Part Two)

Aged 16.

"Andrew, I need a pen."

"What for, dad?"

"To write something down." And wanting to make a lesson of everything, my father added, "Remember when Madeleine gave you her number and you wrote it down?"

"Oh yes."

"Well, Glynnis has three more stanzas. I would like to write them down."

"Oh well, you need a pen."

(Part Three)

Aged 18.

My father was visibly upset. Sitting at the dinner table, I asked him what was wrong.

He didn't even look me in the eye when he answered, "Son, I've found the journal. The family that has it - they don't want to share it with anyone, and they told me to go away and never call again. If you don't mind, I don't want to talk about it."

The only sounds that emitted from that table for the remainder of that dinner, was of stainless steel and china. It was the sound of giving up. Or so I thought.

(Part Four)

Aged 23, I was at work and I received a call from my father. He doesn't even say hello. "Andrew, I need your help, and don't laugh. I have something here. I'm going to read it out to you. Tell me what it is. H –T – T – P - colon. Oh, this is madness."

I said, "Ok dad, it's a web address. Tell me, and I'll load it."

With a vibrato in his voice he said, "Well, what do you see?"

"One second dad, it's loading. Okay, here it comes. The life story of Henry James Kneebone, his complete works."

"How many stanzas are there? Are there three, five, ten? I bet you there's ten stanzas."

"No dad, there's not ten stanzas. Dad, there's 35 pages! You've found it."

"I don't believe you, I don't believe you. I have the first stanza here. You read out your first stanza and we'll see if it matches."

And so I did. *'God ordained that I was born where Cornwall's saintly towers rise, and Newquay's headland like the horn, out between Padstow and St Ives.'* It matched. My father had found this man's story. It was then I needed to know, because I was confused. Why chase Henry's story across two decades?

He answered quite simply. "Son, this man is you. His blood is your blood. Read his story and know that he suffered, and prospered, and use that to give you courage."

(Conclusion)

There are heroes out there, the Olympics, the silver screen, but there are heroes in your own families. If you haven't done so, find their story and read it, and know that they may have suffered but prospered, and use that to give you courage.

Now, as you can imagine, I was stunned, taken aback. But I understood. When it came to courage and perseverance, I didn't learn it from one person, I learned it from two. And for my father, a life's work complete, he was able to have the last words of Henry's poem written on the last resting place of my father.

'So the summer of our life is gone, and the sun is setting in the West. When to this world we are unknown, God grant that may with Him rest.'

(Note: You can access Henry Kneebone's complete poem at: http://freepages.genealogy.rootsweb.ancestry.com/~cornwall/ henrypoem.htm)

CHAPTER 2:
Topic Selection

Tip #5: Choose a single, inspirational core theme rooted in an eternal truth

Contest master George Yen prepared the audience for the next speaker: "Our second contestant is Stuart Pink. Brain Lifting. Brain Lifting. Stuart Pink."

Stuart confidently took the stage in familiar Toastmasters contest attire—a dark suit and an eye-catching yellow tie. He is a physically fit, clean-shaven man with a gentle smile that nicely complements his British accent and affect. After pausing expertly to make eye contact with multiple sections of the audience, Stuart broke into a jog while asking: "Do you like running? Do you belong to a gym, like fifty million Americans do?" Returning to center stage, he switched to jumping jacks and continued: "Mister Contest Chair, fellow Toastmasters. Have you ever had that feeling that you're in the wrong place at the wrong time? I don't mean me, I mean you."

Stuart showed his audience how to approach mental fitness with the same gusto that they apply to physical fitness. He did this by sharing three vignettes involving children who demonstrated the three keys to creativity—curiosity, hope, and optimism. By relating Stuart's stories to their own experiences, the audience would rekindle the creativity locked within.

Beyond timing and originality requirements, contestants are free to do and say pretty much anything they want. Even the judging ballot gives speakers little guidance. That said, of the one hundred possible points that can be awarded, thirty points are associated with topic selection. The first fifteen points are devoted to "Effectiveness: Achievement of Purpose, Interest, Reception" and another fifteen to "Speech Value: Ideas, Logic, Original Thought."

Interestingly, the "Purpose" part of the "Achievement of Purpose" is not defined in any official rule book. Every (good) speech ever delivered predominantly falls into one of the following categories: educational, inspirational, motivational, or entertaining. Winning Toastmasters World Championship speeches are inspirational at their core. The other elements are there to varying degrees, with entertainment most commonly followed by motivation.

In a nutshell, that means the International Speech Contest calls for a seven-minute secular sermon centered on reminding the audience about an eternal truth or virtue. One often hears of the seven heavenly virtues, but there are scores of virtues that are relevant to our daily lives. I have provided in Table 2.1 a partial list of virtues that make great fodder for inspirational speeches of all kinds.

Action (incl. Drive, Ambition, Risk Taking)	**Honesty (incl. Integrity, Sincerity)**
Authenticity (incl. Individuality, Self-Expression)	**Humility (incl. Modesty, Discretion)**
Balance	**Humor (incl. Joyfulness)**
Calm (incl. tranquility)	**Justice (incl. Fairness, Impartiality)**
Charity (incl. Generosity, Sharing, Benevolence)	**Knowledge (incl. Wisdom, Perspective)**
Companionship (incl. Friendship)	**Leadership**
Compassion (incl. Understanding, Acceptance, Tolerance, Empathy, Warmth, Caring)	**Love (incl. Kindness, Appreciation, Faithfulness, Loyalty, Devotion)**
Connectedness (incl. Cooperation, Community)	**Mindfulness (incl. Perspective, Presence, Silence)**
Contentment	**Optimism (incl. Hopefulness, Enthusiasm, Positivity)**
Confidence (incl. Assertiveness)	**Passion (incl. Enthusiasm, Vitality)**
Courage (incl. Valor, Bravery)	**Perseverance (incl. Resilience, Persistence, Industriousness, Determination)**
Creativity (incl. Ingenuity, Originality)	**Responsibility (incl. Citizenship, Trust, Integrity)**
Curiosity (incl. Learning)	**Self-Control (incl. Temperance, Patience)**
Forgiveness (incl. Mercy)	**Spirituality (incl. Faith, Belief)**
Gratitude (incl. Politeness, Courtesy)	**Vulnerability**

Table 2.1: Eternal virtues for inspirational speech topic selection

In the seventeen-year period from 1995 to 2011, variations on the theme of "Love" were the most popular, appearing five times. "Perseverance" was the second most common, having been re-visited three times. "Mindfulness" and "Action" have each found their way to the stage twice. Rounding out the list with one appearance each were: "Compassion," "Creativity," "Self-Expression," "Hope," and "Tolerance."

Any of these themes are fair game if you are a lone speaker inspiring an audience. However, if you are in a speaking contest, you are going to have a much harder time standing out if you speak about love, perseverance, mindfulness, or action.

To our second contestant Stuart Pink's credit, he zigged when others zagged by selecting "Creativity" as his core theme. This theme had not been used as a primary theme since Brett Rutledge won in 1998. Mr. Rutledge shared his challenging personal experiences as a dreamer during his childhood and adolescence. In school, he lived his life in detention because his teachers valued knowledge over imagination. He reminded his audience that the achievements of John F. Kennedy, Martin Luther King, and Albert Einstein would not have been possible if each had not stoked the fire of his imagination and dared to dream.

Tip #6: Limit overly technical subject matter

World Champions generally avoid explaining technical subject matter because it takes time away from storytelling. But, a few examples exist. David Henderson provided the following explanation during his speech:

Many of you are wondering the same thing I wondered. What's sickle cell? It's a genetic blood disorder. People think of it as an African American disease, but it affects people all over the world, from the Middle East to Asia to South America. People with sickle cell have deformed red blood cells, which carry oxygen through your blood vessels. Normal cells look like disks and pass freely through your blood vessels. Sickle cells look like sickles. They clump together causing traffic jams, which in turn cause episodes. First you're fine and then you get an infection and then you're fine and then you're in pain and then you're fine and then you die. There is no known cure.

From prior practice, David likely knew that many of his audience members would know neither the nature nor the expected outcome of a disease that afflicted one of the principal characters in his story. Technical explanations are risky, but there are several best practices that make them safer. First and foremost, practice your explanation in front of diverse audiences to ensure it is compact and clear. Second, consider using an accessible visual metaphor as David did in referring to "traffic jams." Third, add emotional depth to the explanation. David did this by showing the disease was universal. In addition, the phrase "and then you die" created tension by foreshadowing the passing of his best friend.

Though David did not do so in his explanation of sickle cell anemia, speakers occasionally reference large numbers. As David did with his traffic jam metaphor, presenters must transform statistics from the logical to the emotional. The traffic jam metaphor works because it is something that causes daily pain to almost every individual in the audience. The other common tactic for making numbers emotionally resonant is to reduce the scale to the personal level. For example, at the beginning of his speech, Stuart Pink asked, "Do you belong to a gym, like fifty million Americans do?" He could have made his question somewhat more emotionally powerful by asking, "Do you belong to a gym like one in six Americans?"

Brain Lifting

Central message(s)	Creativity
Duration	6.5 minutes
Words per minute	104
Laughs per minute	1.23

Table 2.1: Vital statistics for *Brain Lifting* by Stuart Pink

(Introduction)

Do you like running? Do you belong to a gym, like fifty million Americans do? Mister Contest Chair, fellow Toastmasters. Have you ever had that feeling that you're in the wrong place at the wrong time? I don't mean me, I mean you.

Statistically, you shouldn't be here today. Your ancestors faced countless obstacles. War. Disease. The British Empire. Yet against all the odds, and this early start, you made it here today. You are truly a miracle.

But, what makes us different from all other life? Creativity. Everything you do is a result of creativity. This century will be the creative century. Why do we spend so much time exercising our bodies and not our brains? We need a crash course in thinking and creative fitness, and I like to call it—brain lifting.

(Part 1)

Now, my son Jonathan, when he's not busy being Batman, likes to do jigsaw puzzles. On his fourth birthday, we got him one with 101 pieces. I'll never forget his reaction. "I'm trying to be strong Daddy, so I can do the puzzle." You see, Jonathan is a brain lifter. He knows how to exercise his creative muscle.

How can you become a brain lifter? Why not use the two most important words in the English language. Without these two tiny words, our world would not exist. Do you want to hear what they are? Say yes. [Audience: Yes!]

"What if?" Every great question that has advanced civilization started with "What if?" What if we could fly? What if we could walk on the moon? What if we could speak for five to seven minutes without um-ing or ah-ing?

(Part 2)

As a teacher, I once asked my second-grade class for ideas for a class reward. Abby put her hand up. "Mr. Pink, Mr. Pink, can we go to Italy?"

"Italy? No. We can't go to Italy!"

"Mr. Pink, what if we could?" Abby was brain lifting. A few days later, we transformed the classroom into Venice, and I don't just mean it was underwater because of the leaking roof in the English rain. We learned Italian. We made pizza. We sang "O

Sole Mio." Brain lifting can be fun. But. what if brain lifting could change your life?

(Part 3)

A boy, I'll call him Jack, was bottom of my class. He was always getting into trouble. At home, he suffered from emotional abuse and neglect.

One lunch time, instead of going out with all the other boys, he came in to my chess club and said, "Mr. Pink, what if I could learn chess?"

Now, he was no nerd. As I taught him, he discovered he had a real talent for it. He started to change. His confidence grew, and at the end of the year, he won our chess tournament, beating all the really bright kids.

Brain lifting showed Jack what he was capable of. Do you know what you're capable of? What if it's more? Your brain can think at 268 miles an hour, and that makes you ten times faster than Usain Bolt. Go on, give yourself a gold medal. If you take thinking and you raise it up to that Olympic level, you have the philosophy, but we can all do it.

(Conclusion)

When I asked my class one day. "What if this is just a dream?," they debated it for an hour.

Eight-year-old Jenny said, "When I'm awake, I do things I can do. But when I'm dreaming, I do things I can't do."

Wow. What if you started dreaming more in real life? At the end of that debate, five children in my class actually thought they were in a dream, a bit like me right now. All of these kids reminded me of the power of "what if." They were my teacher.

So, next time you have a problem, do some brain lifting. Next time you face a challenge, ask yourself, "What if?" Next time you have a dream, ask yourself, "What if?" No matter what obstacles you face, there is no wrong place. There is no wrong time to ask... [Audience: "What if?"]

CHAPTER 3:
Storytelling

Tip #7: Relive your epiphany

After the required one minute of silence passed for the judges to record their final impressions of Stuart Pink, the contest master introduced the next speaker, "Our third contestant is Ronald E. Melvin. Disaster to Laughter. Disaster to Laughter. Ronald E. Melvin."

After two Anglo-Saxons, Ronald was the first person of color to take the stage. Over the course of the day, the audience would discover that two-thirds of the finalists were non-White. But, this fact likely went completely unnoticed because Toastmasters International has what is likely the most diverse membership of any top-tier service organization.

Toastmasters is gender-blind—52 percent of members are female and 48 percent are male. Toastmasters is age-blind—the average member age is 45.8 years, but 25 percent of members are eighteen to twenty-four. Toastmasters is income-blind, education-blind, and disability-blind. The same goes for race, religion, and sexual orientation.

At the club level, every person is welcome as long as the individual has an interest in improving his or her public speaking and leadership skills. This diversity extends as a matter of course to the International Speech Contest. In the twenty-five-year period between 1986 and 2011, half of the World Champions were non-White.

Though the root cause has not been determined, the only flaw in Toastmasters' otherwise warm embrace is that only two women have taken home the top prize. The 1990 Toastmaster World Champion, David Brooks, was puzzled by this too and went on the record with a partial theory. Having watched several hundred club-level contests over more than two decades, he observed a ratio of four or five male competitors to every female. With that ratio at the top of the funnel, one would have expected at least four female winners since 1986. For now, the explanation for the remaining underrepresentation remains a mystery.

Centered on his relationship with his white, Jewish best friend Steve Eisenberg, Ronald's speech was a snapshot of the Toastmasters' diversity experience in miniature. Learning from Steve's reactions to increasingly challenging circumstances, Ronald has a revelation tied to the core virtue of positivity. He learns to respond to disaster with laughter. Reliving a personal epiphany is among the very best ways to tell an inspirational story.

Tip #8: Grab attention, reveal your theme, and preview your structure in the opening

While the first contestant started with a story and the second contestant started with a shocking statement, Ronald E. Melvin opened with an audience-participation exercise that is known to magicians as David Copperfield's arm-twist illusion.

Here is how the illusion works. Ronald first asked his audience members to extend their right arm with their thumb pointing up, palm inside. Next he asked them to point their thumb down toward the ground; given human anatomy, the only way to do this comfortably is with a counterclockwise rotation. Once the audience members complied, he then had them bring their left hand over their right hand and lock their fingers together with both thumbs pointing down.

While the audience members remained with their hands clasped, Ronald used clever misdirection to slightly alter his hand position. Unlocking his hands, he pointed to an audience member and said, "Yeah, you got it right." With the audience distracted, he put his hands back together in a way that seemed the same. However, he actually rotated his right hand clockwise then brought his left hand over the right to lock fingers. Asking the audience to follow along on the count of three, he rotated his interlocked hands counterclockwise so that his thumbs were facing up.

Surprised audience members, with their hands unable to rotate, let out their first big laugh just twenty-two seconds into the speech. Ronald would pile on another twenty-one laughs over the course of his six and a half minutes on stage, more than any other speaker in the contest. This is all the more impressive given that Ronald's story grew increasingly dark as he progressed. If you are going to give a speech about turning disaster into laughter, then you had better be funny.

In a happy speech or a sad speech, the first laugh is the critical one since it relaxes the audience and lets them know that they are going to be taken on an emotional journey. Moreover, that first laugh has the added benefit of dramatically lowering the speaker's initial anxiety.

With the laugh under his belt, Ronald revealed his core message by linking his magic trick with the audience's broader life experience: "Sometimes you start out doing something innocent and you end up all twisted. All of those events don't have to be that way. Sometimes we can change disaster into laughter." If there is one nit to pick, it is that getting one's arms twisted is a tenuous metaphor for real-life disasters.

When you join Toastmasters, one of the first things you learn is the mantra "tell 'em what you are going to tell 'em; tell 'em; tell 'em what you told 'em." Less experienced speakers take this literally and give away all the goods in the introduction. For example, they might say: "Today, you will learn the three keys to accomplishing every goal you set for yourself. The keys are planning, persistence, and positivity. First, let's turn our attention to planning." That approach, of course, is just too obvious.

More experienced Toastmasters turn the first part of the mantra into "tease 'em what you are going to tell 'em." This is done by directly revealing the structure and by sharing implicitly or explicitly why your audience should care about what you are about to say. Using the same example, the more proficient speaker shortens the above to, "Today, you will learn the three keys to accomplishing every goal you set for yourself. First, let's turn our attention to the first key—planning." This approach keeps the audience members in suspense while they simultaneously listen and await the satisfying unveiling of the next two keys to success.

The most advanced Toastmasters go one step further. They know that the audience subconsciously forms an expectation of the structure of the speech from the way the speaker opens. By doing a magic trick, one might logically have expected that Ronald would have used additional illusions to metaphorically demonstrate the lessons in his talk. Instead, he shifted into story-telling mode, which made his introduction feel a bit disconnected from the remainder of his speech.

Tip #9: Open with a personal story, a compelling question, or a shocking statement

Ronald took a calculated risk by opening his speech with a magic trick. In the prior twenty-six years, no contest winner had ever done so. His approach was both unique and memorable. But would it score points with the judges?

The safe route would have been to open with a story, as nineteen speakers in that time span had done. Safer still would have been to start with a personal story, the approach of choice for fourteen champions. (The remaining five told stories about others.) Beginning with a story is a very efficient way to let your audience know the underlying structure of your speech. Beginning with a personal story has the added benefit of building an immediate emotional connection.

Take, for example, the 2007 World Champion, Vikas Jhingran, who allowed his audience to relive one of the defining moments of his life:

My hands were shaking. My throat was dry. In my hand was a letter that was going to change my life. Would it be for the better or worse? The answer was inside. I stared at the return address, MIT, Massachusetts Institute of Technology, the graduate school of my dreams. Would it begin with congratulations or 'you've got to be kidding.' The answer was inside.

Surprisingly, five previous winners opened with *someone else's* story. In 2009, Mark Hunter conjured Don Quixote, the man of La Mancha, to personify what it means to idealistically champion the rights of others. Though he quickly shifted to personal storytelling in the body of his speech, he integrated subtle chivalric references throughout his speech, including references to a lance, armor, and a horse. His approach of using repeated symbols, known in screenwriting theory as a thematic image system, added depth and sophistication.

Nevertheless, telling non-personal stories is otherwise a relic of bygone times. In 1986, Arabella Bengson opened with

Pygmalion. In 1987, Harold Patterson opened with an exchange between the artists Henri Matisse and Pierre-Auguste Renoir. In 1991, David Ross described a metaphysical train that transports people to success. In 1993, Otis Williams Jr. referenced Thomas Edison. Only the earliest two, Ms. Bengson and Mr. Patterson, never transitioned into personal storytelling. It would be hard to believe that such impersonal speeches could win today.

After storytelling, the next most popular opening is a provocative question. The champions in 2011, 2005, 2001, and 1992 took this approach. In fact, the 2005 winner, Lance Miller, even titled his speech 'The Ultimate Question." He connected getting your parking ticket validated with empowering others by expressing appreciation for their strengths rather than focusing on their weaknesses. He began:

The ultimate question, that question that has plagued man since the dawn of time and that question that each and every one of us must ask at some point in our life, do you validate?

Though you see many speakers today open with quotes, it is no longer considered a sophisticated approach. People want to hear your words. It is, however, still acceptable to include quotes within the body of a speech. The last time a speech that opened with a quote won the International Speech Contest was in 1995, when Mark Brown used "You never get a second chance to make a first impression." The only other instance was in 1990, when

David Brooks quoted the title of Thomas Wolfe's novel *You Can't Go Home Again.*

Outside of stories, questions, and quotes, there is only one type of opener that has not appeared in winning Toastmasters speeches—the shocking statement. As there is no example in the realm of the Toastmasters contest, let's turn to the world of the TED Conference.

Shocking statements most frequently rely on statistics. However, they can also express strong opinions that challenge conventional wisdom. The important thing is that your point must trigger a range of audience emotions. If you share a "what," then people will have a burning need to fill in the gaps on why, how, when, and where. In his TED2010 talk, celebrity chef and child-nutrition advocate Jamie Oliver used exactly this recipe in his opening. Listen to how he started:

Sadly, in the next eighteen minutes when I do our chat, four Americans that are alive will be dead from the food that they eat. My name is Jamie Oliver. I am thirty-four years old. I am from Essex in England and for the last seven years I have worked fairly tirelessly to save lives in my own way. I am not a doctor; I'm a chef. I don't have expensive equipment, or medicine. I use infor- mation and education. I profoundly believe that the power of food has a primal place in our homes that binds us to the best bits of life.

Chef Oliver captured his audience by sharing what is happen- ing—people are dropping like flies from the food they eat. And, they are not halfway around the world in a developing country; they are in the same modern nation as his audience. No doubt most of the audience members were wondering if they would survive lunch! Such is the power of a shocking statistic that is deeply and personally relevant to the audience. People have four core needs: physical health and safety; love and belonging; desire and self-interest; and hope in a brighter future. Jamie went primal, life and death, and had his audience waiting with bated breath to find out why this is happening and to learn how to stay alive.

Tip #10: Make your transitions crystal clear

Ronald completed the last sentence of his introduction—"Sometimes we can change disaster into laughter"—and then signaled his transition into the body of his speech in multiple ways.

First, he took a two-second pause. Throughout this book, the pause will appear countless times, since it plays innumerable roles in great speaking. Pauses at transition points allow audience members to compartmentalize and digest the prior part of your speech and prepare their brains for new material.

Second, he moved several steps to his left as he began to share a personal story about living in Rochester, Minnesota, in the 1980s. As I will discuss in depth later in the book, movement on stage should be choreographed the same way that movement is orchestrated in live theater. Ronald's movement appeared frenetic and unstructured. In fact, moving left just a few steps rather than a significant distance was evidence of this.

During his speech, Ronald covered three vignettes that occurred at different times and different physical locations. Hence, he had two options. He could have mapped the stage chronologically. This is the most common approach in Toastmasters and beyond. Since Western audiences read left to right, he should have started his story by moving to the audience's left rather than to his left. His second option would have been to lay out the stage like a map. This would have been more challenging, though not impossible, given that his locations were Minnesota, an airplane, and Florida.

In addition to pausing and moving, there are additional ways to clearly signal your speech transition. Ronald demonstrated one of them well and the other not as well. The one he did nicely was using language that indicates a turning point. He began the first part of the body of his speech with, "It was the 1980s; I was living in Rochester, Minnesota." Any major shift in plot, setting, time, or character signals a transition. In addition, there is a wide range of words and phrases that have just as strong an impact. Here are just a few examples. A speaker can use "however" to illustrate contrast, "generally speaking" to move from a narrow example to a larger point, or "next" to indicate the next item in a sequence.

Ronald's only missed opportunity to signal a transition was that he did not noticeably shift his vocal delivery. Throughout the speech, he maintained a passionate conversational style that was generally loud, fast, and accentuated by pauses. Transitions are most effective when they have a large contrast. Hence, Ronald could have shifted his voice to slower and softer during the transition. In spite of that, with all the other best practices he applied, the audience had no doubt that he had moved from the introduction into the body of his speech.

Tip #11: Build a logical narrative structure by choosing the variety and progression of stories

All great speeches have an introduction, body, and conclusion. Beyond that constraint, there are endless opportunities to creatively build the narrative structure for a speech.

In broad brush strokes, Ronald Melvin constructed his speech in the following way. In his introduction, Ronald delivered a problem statement—sometimes life throws us challenges and we need to choose how to respond. The body of his speech consisted of three distinct stories. The first story is set in the 1980s, when the speaker attends his friend Steve's wedding. The point of this story is that we can turn embarrassment into laughter. The second story, set slightly later in time, relates Ronald's experience of riding in Steve's airplane. The point of this story is that we can turn accidents into laughter. The third story recounts Ronald's experience at the end of Steve's life. The point of this story is that we can turn tragedy into laughter. Finally, he concluded by driving home his core message:

"Les Brown says, 'If you get knocked down, get knocked down on your back so you can see which way to get up.' I say to you, when you get up, get up laughing and turn disaster into laughter."

Beyond the risk he took in opening with a magic trick—which could equally have helped him or hurt him—Ronald's speech was extremely well constructed. He made a clear choice to tell three separate stories that were cobbled together by virtue of many best practices. The stories were chronologically linear in time. Each of the stories had the same characters. And, most elegantly, the stories reinforced the theme of turning disaster into laughter in increasingly high-stakes situations.

Looking back on the seventeen-year period between 1995 and 2011, Ronald was in good company in terms of telling multiple stories. During that time period, winners told a single story three times, two stories four times, three stories seven times, and four stories three times. This shows there is no hard-and-fast rule about the quantity of stories.

At this point, you may be wondering how to differentiate between a speech with three separate stories and a speech with a single story told in three acts. Though there is no official distinction, modern storytelling experts Joseph Campbell, Christopher Vogler, and Robert McKee provide some insight on what a complete, three-act story looks like.

Typically, Act 1 introduces the protagonist in his ordinary world. We get to know the essential details of his abilities, his mind-set, his desires, his relationships, and his flaws. The first act ends and Act 2 begins with an inciting incident that casts the protagonist on a journey of escalating intrapersonal, interpersonal, or extrapersonal (e.g., societal) conflict. The second act ends and Act 3 begins at the resolution of an explosive climax representing the protagonist's ultimate challenge. In Act 3, loose ends are closed and we see the protagonist at home in his new world, transformed physically, morally, or more often, emotionally.

Some readers may be more familiar with the "Pixar Pitch" espoused by Matthew Luhn, head of story at the acclaimed animation studio. Here is an overlay of that technique on the three-act narrative structure. The ordinary world in Act 1 maps to "Once upon a time... And every day..." The next part, "Until one day...," is the inciting incident that bridges Act 1 to Act 2. The progressive complications of Act 2 are Pixar's "And because of that... And because of that... And because of that..." The climax begins with "Until finally..." The story then concludes with the new normal world and the illumination of the core message, "And since that day... And the moral of the story is..."

Let's deconstruct Ronald's first story to illustrate why it is indeed a story and not simply a first act. In Ronald's ordinary world, he is the lone person of color living in Rochester, Minnesota during the 1980s. The good news is that he has made a great friend, Steve, whom he first met at a business meeting. Act 1 ends and Act 2 begins innocuously enough when Ronald is invited to Steve's wedding. Hilarity ensues when the bride and groom are announced as Mr. and Mrs. Jackson. The problem is that Steve's last name is Eisenberg! The tension reaches its climax at the end of Act 2 when Ronald reclaims his gift from the Jackson party's table. Act 3 establishes a new normal of close friendship and laughter between Ronald and Steve. With all conflict resolved and the moral of turning disaster into laughter fully revealed, the first story is complete.

Story variety is just one lever at the speaker's disposal. The other lever is story progression, which is simply a way of thinking about the chronological flow of a story or a sequence of stories. The four types of story progression include: linear, independent, flashback, and nonlinear.

By telling his stories in standard chronological order, Ronald delivered a textbook example of a linear progression. Past world champions delivered their speeches using a strict linear progression six times between 1995 and 2011. Those speakers included Mark Hunter in 2009, LaShunda Rundles in 2008, Edward Hearn in 2006, Lance Miller in 2005, Randy Harvey in 2004, and Ed Tate in 2000.

The independent story progression was equally common, with six instances between 1995 and 2011. In this type, the speaker tells multiple stories that have no obvious chronological progression. In fact, the independent stories need not share any core elements such as characters or setting. However, they must share the speech's central message as a theme.

By way of illustration, consider the independent narrative structure of Mark Brown's speech from 1995. Mark leads off with the aphorism "We never get a second chance to make a first impression." The body of his speech has two independent stories. With one less story than is typical, Mr. Brown was able to provide significantly more detail in his remaining stories. In the first, he recounts the plot elements of Disney's "Beauty and the Beast" to illustrate that intolerance, ignorance, and indifference are alive and well in the world of fantasy. In his second story, Mr. Brown described how NBC television news anchor Pat Harper spent five days living as a homeless person on the icy streets of New York City in January 1995. Though independent with respect to characters, setting, time, and even reality, these stories highlighted that intolerance, ignorance, and indifference were alive and well in the real world. Mark concluded his speech by asking the audience members to look at themselves in the mirror so that they would henceforth remember to give others a second chance.

The flashback story progression is a variation on the linear theme and was used by Vikas Jhingran in 2007 and by David Henderson in 2010. Of the two instances, Mr. Jhingran's is the more prototypical example.

In the introduction, we find Mr. Jhingran holding an unopened decision letter from MIT, the graduate school of his dreams. The audience is left at this Act 1 cliffhanger with the words "the answer was inside.'" Vikas transitions into the body of his speech and linearly progresses through a three-story flashback that includes two visits to a Swami during his teenage years and a mind-altering epiphany during his freshman year at college. Over the course of the stories, Mr. Jhingran realizes that the answer to his struggles in school also lies inside. Finally, his conclusion does double duty. First, Vikas delivers Act 2 and Act 3 of his initial story by revealing that the letter offered congratulations. Second, he asks the audience members to look inside themselves for the answers to their problems.

David Henderson's speech is a noteworthy variation of the flashback progression. Whereas Mr. Jhingran started his story, turned the clock back, then returned chronologically, David used an embedded flashback purely for character development.

David's story begins as he and his childhood best friend Jackie Parker are pretending to be fighter pilots trying to defeat the Red Baron—the decorated World War I German fighter pilot and Snoopy's nemesis. The body of David's speech begins with a flashback designed to reveal the emotional bond formed when he met Jackie at a kindergarten Halloween contest. Note that there was no inciting incident at the end of the introductory fighter pilot vignette. David simply reversed the chronological order of two pieces that establish the ordinary world in Act 1 of his story. David's speech transitions into Act 2 by returning to the end of the fighter pilot scene when Jackie falls down, recovers too slowly, and is diagnosed with sickle cell anemia. Sadly, Jackie passes away at the climax of Act 2. In Act 3, David is transformed to his new normal when he overcomes his fear of death and accepts that losing people is part of loving people.

Though several world champions—especially in earlier years—blended linear and independent stories, only one successfully claimed victory with the nonlinear progression. This approach is artful but carries the risk of appearing chaotic. In addition, it is also extremely challenging for the storyteller to keep straight in his mind. Using cinematic references, one nonlinear approach is the reverse chronology of Christopher Nolan's 2000 film "Memento." A more complex version is Quentin Tarantino's 1994 story weave in "Pulp Fiction."

The 2001 Toastmasters champion, Darren LaCroix, was victorious with Tarantino's method. He began his speech by acting out a dramatic statement of a common problem that people face—we give up too quickly when faced with adversity. He supported this issue with Act 1 of his first story when he went into debt after buying a Subway sandwich shop. Next, he delivered Act 1 of his second story about rocket pioneer Robert Goddard. In short order, he shared Act 1 of his third story, a personal vignette about his desire to become a comedian. Next, he successively delivered Act 2 of the Goddard story, Act 2 and Act 3 of the comedian story, Act 2 and Act 3 of the Subway story, and then Act 3 of the Goddard story. To recap, that weave is story 1, 2, 3, 2, 3, 1, 2. Finally, he concluded by asking his audience to take the next step, demonstrating that you still make progress even when you fail. Though his nonlinear progression was extremely complex, or perhaps because of it, he delivered what is widely regarded to be one of the best Toastmasters speeches of all time.

Tip #12: Create archetypal characters, including a protagonist, a mentor, and an opponent

Even if you have great narrative structure (also known as plot), your speech needs characters that fit squarely into the archetypical roles listeners expect to meet. Adhering to conventional character types amplifies emotional impact. The audience naturally yearns for the hero to succeed and hates the villain for getting in the hero's way. Moreover, these archetypes are critical time savers.

The primary role in every story is the protagonist. Because of this, introduce the hero to your audience as the first character they meet at the beginning of your story. Ronald, along with the overwhelming majority of past Toastmasters champions, told his stories from the first-person perspective. Over the course of Ronald's stories, the audience got a picture of his strengths, his desires, and his flaws—the three elements of character development. As for strengths, we know that he is both compassionate and sociable. By mentioning with a humorous tone that he was the lone person of color in a city of 110,000, he reveals his desire to fit in. His flaw links to the core message; Ronald, like most people, gets anxious in the face of disaster.

There is one great danger in telling personal stories: putting yourself on a pedestal. This can happen in many subtle and not so subtle ways. Many amateur speakers share their bona fides in a heavy-handed way, for example, by rattling off their impressive biography at the start of their talk.

There are less obvious and often unintentional ways, though, for a speaker to raise himself above an audience. In an honest desire to appear authoritative and confident, some speakers fail to reveal vulnerability and thus lose an important way to bond with the audience; they fail to generate empathy. The second way is by telling stories where the author makes it through an epic struggle all on their own. That might sound admirable, but the audience members can only connect if they believe that they can achieve the same success the speaker achieved. To make that connection, the speaker should persevere with a special process. The speaker must not be special; the speaker must have a special process that he or she reveals to the audience as the story progresses.

The speaker can acquire a special process either by developing it on his or her own or by obtaining it from a mentor. Though both approaches are effective, gaining a special process from a mentor is almost always the better way. By discovering a special recipe for success organically, the speaker will seem smarter, stronger, and faster than the average bear. In learning the process from a wise mentor, the speaker is eye-to-eye, heart-to-heart with the audience. Just as the speaker gained a valuable gift from someone else, the speaker pays that gift forward to the audience.

Ronald Melvin clearly had this principle in mind when he chose his friend, Steve Eisenberg, as his mentor. Steve showed Ronald how to laugh in the face of disaster, even in Steve's darkest hour. Just as Luke Skywalker had Obi-Wan Kenobi in Star Wars, Ronald had Steve. And, just as Luke had to lose his mentor, Ronald had to lose Steve to stand on his own and be able to laugh in the face of future disaster.

Mentors come in all forms in Toastmasters speeches. Mostly, they are family, including mothers, grandmothers, fathers, and children. Frequently, they are friends. However, there have been exotic mentors as well.

Though now considered cliché, it was not uncommon for speakers in the past to architect stories using major historical figures as mentors. In 1998, Brett Rutledge referenced John F. Kennedy, Martin Luther King, and Einstein as examples of people who ignored the establishment and dared to dream. In 2001, Darren LaCroix drew inspiration from rocketry pioneer Robert Goddard to show what people can achieve if they refuse to give up.

Mentors need not be human beings. They can be inanimate objects. Ed Hearn, the 2006 champion, learned how to bounce back from a weighed bowl that he extracted from a child's inflatable punching bag. Another clever example was Willie Jones's mentor in his 1997 speech—a computer that taught him how to press control-alt-delete on his past regrets.

The most exotic mentors are intangible. In 2002, Dwayne Smith shared a touching story about how music instilled life-saving hope when his friend was at the brink of suicide. The 1995 champion, Mark Brown used a cartoon character from Disney's "Beauty and the Beast" to dramatize intolerance. And, in a moment of creative brilliance, Craig Valentine brought his own wise yet sarcastic reflection to life to teach Craig the benefit of mindfulness enabled by silence.

Well-developed protagonists and mentors are enough to make a good story. But to make a great story, there must be an opponent, introduced early on, who is hated deeply by the audience. With the exception of Brett Rutledge's rally against teachers and "the establishment," the villains in winning Toastmasters speeches have always been intangible evils. These evils are the foil to the core message of the speech. When the speech inspires people to persevere, the opponent is fear. For action, it is complacency. For love and compassion, it is intolerance, discrimination, or simply rudeness. Since audiences and judges expect to be inspired, the opponent must always be defeated in the end. There is no sequel.

In the worlds of movies and literature, there are many other character types, such as tricksters, false allies, and false opponents. However, with disqualification looming at seven minutes and thirty-one seconds, there are generally no "extras" in the International Speech Contest.

Tip #13: Bring your characters to life with dialogue, physical presence, and voice

To bring characters to life, the speaker cannot simply retell stories about them. The speaker needs to relive the stories *with* them. The mantra "Don't retell your story, relive your story" is attributed to motivational speaker Lou Heckler and was popularized by Toastmasters World Champion Craig Valentine. In Craig's words, "you've got to invite them into the scene of your story so they can hear it how your heard it, see it how you saw it, and feel how you felt it."

At the minimum, this requires giving characters realistic dialogue. Think about how people converse with their friends. Real dialogue is short. It achieves verisimilitude by breaking the ordinary rules of grammar with contractions, partial sentences, and even the occasional "um," "like," or "you know." It conveys emotion. Though dialogue can be used (very sparingly) to share information, its primary purpose is either to move the story forward or to contribute to revealing a character's strengths, flaws, and desires.

Real dialogue is more powerful when it conveys the subtext, or deeper meaning, of a character's true emotions and desires. In an effort to protect their egos from humiliation, characters are at the

very least vague and often make statements that are contradictory to what they actually want. In addition to beating around the
bush and lying, the other common form of subtext-laden dialogue
involves characters discussing a topic that serves as a symbolic or
metaphorical representation of a looming, unspoken issue.

Ronald's speech has a mixture of dialogue with subtext and
dialogue that is "on the nose." The very first line of dialogue is of
the latter variety: "My name's Steve. I know how you feel. I go and
recruit at minority colleges, and even though I'm treated well, I
still feel uncomfortable." Steve's transparent emotional disclosure did feel somewhat realistic and served to efficiently highlight
a common bond with the speaker. Ronald's response to Steve—
"Welcome to my world!"—was richly laden with the subtext of
what it is like to be a minority. Consider how unrealistic it would
have been for Ronald to respond with "on the nose" dialogue:
"Yes, I am frequently the only African American person in a room
full of Caucasians. That does often make me uncomfortable."

Dialogue with subtext is also one of the key ways to get laughs
from an audience. The wittiest line of dialogue in Ronald's speech
comes when Steve is about to take him up in an airplane and asks:
"Mel, have you ever seen a pencil float?" This line is immediate
foreshadowing. Ronald follows the dialogue with action, another
best practice in storytelling, when he adds: "With that, he grabbed
the controls and pulled it back. The plane went into a climb, it
started coughing and spluttering."

Within reason, each character should have a distinct speech pattern or voice. Drawing on stereotypes, younger characters might speak more slowly and with less-than-crisp enunciation. If the speaker is a woman, she might adopt a lower pitch when delivering male dialogue. If a character is older, then his or her voice may be slightly gruffer. Sometimes, a regional accent is appropriate. This paragraph started with "within reason" for a reason. In most dialogue, each character's voice need only be tailored enough to be distinct. The exception, of course, is over-the-top characters used for comic relief.

One of the mantras of good storytelling is "show, don't tell." That guideline applies to writing dialogue as well. If dialogue explicitly tells what a character is thinking, doing, or feeling, then it is not realistic.

Tip #14: Bring your audience into your setting

Perhaps the biggest mistake that speakers make when telling stories is being too vague about setting. In fact, while I was writing this chapter, a fellow Toastmaster reached out to me seeking feedback on her speech with precisely this problem.

The first couple of lines of her speech were as follows (some details changed to protect the innocent): "Years ago, when I first started to work for the University of Rhodesia as an International Student Advisor, there were only two employees operating the

International Student Office. Every day, I just put my head down and focused on getting the job done. I noticed that my coworker Jane would go into our boss' office at least once a day to discuss a variety of things, both work-related and personal."

To be realistic, to allow the audience to relive the story, setting must be specific in time, location, and atmosphere. In the example above, the speaker is imprecise about time in two ways. First, by using "Years ago," the audience members do not know if it was two years, five years, or ten years. Consequently, they cannot turn the clock back to put themselves at the right point in historical time. Second, by beginning the second sentence with "Every day," the audience cannot picture an exact day. The whole setup is fuzzy.

The speaker did a better job of describing the location—the International Student Office at the University of Rhodesia. But audiences need sensory description to recreate the scene. Could she see Jane's meticulously neat desk? Could she hear the sound of students speaking a Babel of languages? Could she smell and even taste the chalk dust lingering in the air? Could she feel the smoothness of her worn wooden chair arm? Though all of these details need not and should not be provided all at once, the speaker should have provided a few more particulars to bring her audience into her office so that they could emotionally feel what she felt.

Atmosphere, the final element of setting is the key to establishing the mood. Perhaps this example could have been set during the long slow days of summer recess when Jane had nothing better to do than to brownnose with the boss in his air-conditioned, florescent-lit office. Seasons, weather, lighting, and even physical objects carry built-in moods that help the speaker establish setting with fewer words.

Tip #15: Choose messages with universal audience appeal

David Henderson, the 2010 World Champion, advises speakers to be mindful by choosing stories that appeal both to men and to women. Men are particularly guilty of focusing on their father-son experience and of using sports metaphors, something female listeners do not relate to as strongly.

Excluding historical figures, the mentor was female in nearly every winning Toastmasters speech between 1995 and 2011 that had a human mentor. This included mothers, grandmothers, an office receptionist, a young girl, and a television news reporter.

Though Toastmasters audiences and judges are diverse on most every dimension, they do share a common human experience. You cannot go wrong if you share a deep message rooted in an eternal truth embedded in a personal story that is mindful of the perspectives of a diverse audience.

Disaster To Laughter

© 2012 Ronald E. Melvin

Central message(s)	Positivity
Duration	6.58 Minutes
Words per minute	153
Laughs per minute	3.34

Table 3.1: Vital statistics for *Disaster To Laughter* by Ronald E. Melvin

(Introduction)

Would you take your hand and put out in front of you like this, palm inside. Yes, everybody, stick it out there. Very good. Would you now point your thumb down to the ground? Very good. Taking the left hand and placing it over, locking the fingers. Yup, you've got it right, you've got it right. Okay, one, two, three, turn them over. Very good. Contest Chair, Toastmasters and guests. That's life.

Sometimes you start out doing something innocent and you end up all twisted. All of those events don't have to be that way. Sometimes we can change disaster into laughter.

(Part 1)

It was the 1980s. I was living in Rochester, Minnesota. 110,000 people and three of color. Me, myself, and I. I went to a business meeting and a gentleman came up to me and said, "My name's

Steve. I know how you feel. I go and recruit at minority colleges, and even though I'm treated well, I still feel uncomfortable."

I said, "Welcome to my world!" We bonded that time and became very good friends. He invited me to his wedding. Beautiful wedding. I went to the reception just in time to see two young ladies walking in the door. Wine, women and song. They went down the hallway and they had a number of these receptions going on. They went to a table and there were their names, and I saw mine. I picked it up and I followed them in. I went up and I placed my gift there, and went to the assigned table but I was surprised.

All the chairs were taken, but they were so gracious. They parted and the waiter went to get me a chair and I went to the open bar. Well then the announcer started to introduce the bridal party, and he got to the part, and he said "For the first time, we'd like to announce, Mr. and Mrs. Jackson."

"Jackson? Who's Jackson? Steve's name is Eisenberg!" I ran outside and I took a look and in that moment of clarity I saw that the signs were facing opposite ways and I had went [sic] in the wrong door.

Okay, I'll go in the right door. Oh, my gift! Just as I turned around, I looked at the announcer coming out and I explained my situation. He said, "Well, go in and get your gift."

I said, "What's wrong with you Mr. Wilson?"

Well, at this point I said I'm not going in there by myself. He took me in, and I got my gift and I followed him closely back out.

When Steve saw me, he grabbed me and hugged me, said, "Mel, it's so good to see you!" I told him what happened, he began to laugh. Then I told him about the gift. He laughed harder. He had turned disaster into laughter.

(Part 2)

Later on, he took me up in a plane and it was like being in a Volkswagen with wings. As we were up there, I guess he was getting bored because he reached into his pocket, he pulled out a pencil and he placed it on the dash. He said, "Mel, have you ever seen a pencil float?" With that, he grabbed the controls and pulled it back. The plane went into a climb, it started coughing and spluttering. At that point, he shoved the controls and the plane went in a dive. I went from grabbing this to pushing that.

I looked over at Steve and he was knocked out, but it was floating. Folks, that's when I heard that little girl screaming. Yes, it was me. They say your life flashes in front of you. Not mine, it stood perfectly still, except for that little light that said "boy, you're going to die."

At that point the plane started to level off. I looked back at Steve, he was rubbing his head. He finally got the controls, he said, "You know this plane is trained to fly normally when nobody touches the control."

"Yea, thanks for telling me."

Now he brings the plane down to land. Bringing it in to a stop, he reaches down and he notices that his seatbelt had been unhooked. I had done it when I threw my hands up, he had hit his head on the top of the plane. We started to laugh. We laughed. I made the mistake of telling him about the little girl screaming. But anyway, we had turned disaster into laughter.

(Part 3)

I moved to Florida. I tried to get him to come see me, and finally one day, he said, "Mel, I can't. I have Lou Gehrig's disease." This disease robs you of your muscles and your nerves.

A couple of weeks later, I got a call from his wife saying, "If you want to see him, you better come now." I took the first plane to Minnesota, and I walked in the house and there was Steve in this contraption that his wife had to use to lift and move him around the house.

I sat there on the sofa and I started to cry. "Oh, my friend, Steve. Why you?"

Steve said, "Mel, do you remember when you went to the wrong reception?"

"Huh?" He was changing disaster into laughter. We started to laugh about all the bloopers I had done while I was in Rochester, until he couldn't breathe again, and his wife ran over to grab him. I grabbed him and I hugged him as hard as I could because he could not hold me.

(Conclusion)

We can't cure everything with laughter, but we can feel better. Why do we wait until people are gone before we talk about their bloopers? We start off saying something nice, "Oh that Mel looked good up on stage until he fell off."

Les Brown says, "If you get knocked down, get knocked down on your back so you can see which way to get up." I say to you, when you get up, get up laughing and turn disaster into laughter.

CHAPTER 4:
Humor and
Emotional Range

Tip #16: Get the first laugh fast

The next speaker entered the stage confidently in a blue blazer, white shirt with striped tie, and khaki slacks as the contest master announced his name and speech title. "Brian Corey. Keep the Music Alive. Keep the Music Alive. Brian Corey."

After scat-singing a few jazzy, melodic lines, Brian delivered a single line that served to set up his core message and to get his first laugh: "Music has the way to move the spirit, ease the mind, and uplift the soul... even in a room with 3,000 Toastmasters." Just like any social group, Toastmasters are always looking for inside jokes to break the tension of their stereotyped identity. Though he did not get a big laugh, he scored a hearty chuckle just thirty seconds into his speech.

It is worth pausing to ask why humor is so important in public speaking. After all, there was no humor in Abraham Lincoln's 1863 Gettysburg Address or Martin Luther King's 1963 "I Have a Dream" speech. However, these and other speeches deemed to have been the greatest of all time were designed to galvanize, educate, grieve, and inspire hope for a brighter tomorrow. Mostly political, these speeches were crafted to change the destiny of the world.

Until very recently, comic relief was neither expected nor accepted in great oratory, especially during moments of national mourning. However, it is instructive to compare President Reagan's address to the American people following the space shuttle Challenger disaster with that of President Obama following a mass shooting at Sandy Hook Elementary School.

Following the loss of seven astronauts, President Reagan addressed the American citizens with a eulogy that is considered to be one of the greatest speeches in modern American rhetoric. He put space exploration in context as a risky but worthy endeavor that must continue to be pursued. He respectfully acknowledged the grief of the astronauts' families, of the many children who watched the shuttle disintegrate on live television, and of the employees of NASA. His 650-word speech was filled with strong emotion. Hope and perseverance, rather than humor, were the relief valves.

On December 14, 2012, twenty young children and six adults were tragically and seemingly randomly killed at Sandy Hook Elementary School by a heavily armed gunman. President Obama addressed the families, the citizens of Newtown, Connecticut, and the American nation two days later. He offered heartfelt condolences and issued a promise to reform America's lax gun-control standards. About a quarter of the way into his 1,670-word speech,

President Obama allowed listeners to release their pain a little with the following story:

And then there were the scenes of the schoolchildren, helping one another, holding each other, dutifully following instructions in the way that young children sometimes do; one child even trying to encourage a grown-up by saying, "I know karate. So it's okay. I'll lead the way out."

Even in tragedy, we begin the process of healing with laughter. The laughter that people expressed upon hearing this story was the laughter of release.

In venues outside politics and social reform, and especially in Toastmasters contests, the speaker's purpose is to inspire and to entertain. Humor serves both purposes. Inspiration stirs deep emotions and humor is the sugar that helps the medicine to go down. And, it goes without saying that humor is a foundational pillar of entertainment.

At the beginning of a speech, just as the applause melts away, the audience falls into silence and stillness. This change introduces physical and psychological tension in the room. Out of respect, people with a tickle in their throat hold back their cough; people who are uncomfortable in their chair wait to shift their weight. This tension is precisely why getting the first laugh fast is so critical to a winning speech. The audience wants the speaker - no, needs the speaker - to release the pressure valve in the room with humor.

For normal speakers, getting a large audience to laugh in half a minute is a major accomplishment. But, in the World Championship of Public Speaking, seconds matter. The first speaker of the day, Andrew Kneebone, got his first laugh in ninety-five seconds. The second, Stuart Pink, took just twelve. The final speaker of the day scored his first laugh in an impressive seven seconds.

Even by historical World Championship standards, Brian was a little slow off the block. This was mainly due to his decision to start by singing. From 1995 to 2011, the champions earned their first laugh after an average of just twenty-five seconds. The slowest was Jock Elliott at eighty-eight seconds.

The fastest during that time period was Brett Rutledge in 1998 who got his first laugh in just four seconds with "I was the kind of kid your parents told you to not play with." Besides the fact that self-deprecating humor is a nearly foolproof technique, Mr. Rutledge's humor was amplified because it surprised an audience conditioned to expect serious plot and setting development before character development in stories.

Tip #17: Crank up the laughs per minute with superiority, surprise, and release

During the course of his seven-minute-and-nine-second speech, Brian Corey elicited laughter from the audience five times. As previously mentioned, he got his first laugh at the thirty-second mark by helping Toastmasters to laugh at themselves. He got additional laughs at forty-six seconds, at one minute and twenty-seven seconds, at two minutes and twenty-six seconds, and at six minutes and twenty seconds. This worked out to 0.7 laughs per minute.

Though not necessarily removing him from contention on the winner's platform, this low density of humor certainly put Brian at a disadvantage. He, in fact, had drawn the least number of laughs of any competitor in the 2012 finals.

In the seventeen years between 1995 and 2011, World Champions averaged an impressive 2.5 laughs per minute. Even the least humorous winner, Mark Brown in 1995, averaged just over one joke per minute. The second-lowest was Dwayne Smith in 2002, who averaged 1.4 laughs per minute. You might think that speeches with music as a major component are simply less funny since that is a common thread between Mr. Brown's, Mr. Smith's, and Brian's speeches. However, the 2009 champion, LaShunda Rundles, also delivered a music-rich speech with a respectable 2.4 laughs per minute; that is all the more impressive when you consider that her speech also delved deeply into incurable illness and death. Any speech can be made funnier with focus. (Tragically, Ms. Rundles passed away at the age of forty-two from the illness about which she spoke, lupus, on August 21, 2012.)

In order to understand how to get more laughs per minute, we must first delve into the psychology of laughter. At present, there is no grand unified theory of why people laugh. Instead, there are three explanations that are complementary and overlapping. The first theory of why humans laugh is to claim superiority. A great deal of humor falls squarely into this category, including laughing at people who make bad decisions or are eccentric. This type of humor is amplified when the person is in a position of authority and when he fits a particular stereotype—some politically correct and some not. Superiority-based humor has an escalating scale of viciousness, starting with gentle parody and satire, moving to moderate sarcasm, and progressing to scathing insults.

With fair warning that deconstructing humor destroys it, consider Brian's lead-off laugh. His joke implies that Toastmasters take themselves too seriously and are neither light of spirit, nor mind, nor soul. Being a Toastmaster himself, he is self-deprecating. Additionally, his quip delivers the subtlest of insults directed at the audience from one of their own. Hence, the audience is made to simultaneously feel superior and inferior.

The laugh Brian received at two minutes and twenty-six seconds is also partially explained by the superiority theory. Referring to a period during college when he struggled to balance schoolwork and music practice, Brian shared the following vignette:

I was at a moment in my life where I needed some encouragement. What better place to go than [to] my academic advisor. I knew he would fold his arms, lean back in his chair and say, 'Son, we've all been there. Stick with this. You can do it.' Boy was I wrong. The message he gave me was life changing. I can sum it up in one word [PAUSE]: 'Quit!'

From the point of view of a college student in trouble, an academic advisor was a strong authority figure. The advisor's counsel was life-changing for the impressionable mind. And yet, this particular advisor gave unexpectedly bad advice. In doing so, he gave a future audience the chance to cut him down with laughter.

The bad advice given to Brian in that joke works on another level. It evokes surprise, the second theory of why humans laugh. A short list of humor accounted for by this theory includes: sheer absurdity; bad advice; exaggeration or farce; irony; puns or plays on words; screwball comedy; physical comedy; and the cousins of overstatement and understatement. People are delightfully surprised by witty incongruity or heavy shock.

Brian scored two of his five laughs from physical comedy. The first was at forty-six seconds, when he said, "At church there was music." Just after saying the words "at church...," he squatted down, raised his arms, and shook his hands in the stereotyped, demonstrative style of the Christian evangelical movement. The second laugh from physical comedy, at six minutes and twenty seconds, joined the King of Pop's signature leg-kick dance move with the line: "There is something inside that only you can provide. Just like Mozart, Beethoven, Michael Jackson gave us music, you have something extraordinary."

The third theory is that people laugh to release strong emotions. Often, laughter is a salve to the darker emotions of embarrassment and fear. Gallows, or morbid, humor is explained well by this theory; we laugh to dismiss fears of our own mortality. Similarly, laughing at scatological or sexual humor relieves embarrassment.

Emotional release explains the remaining laugh of Brian's we have the pleasure of deconstructing. At one minute and twenty-seven seconds, Brian shares the following about his fellow college students: "I would often look at my classmates and they seemed to have plenty of time to study and P-A-R-T-Y." The small dance he did when saying the word "party' could be explained as purely physical comedy. However, it also allows the release of good feelings for many, and embarrassment for some, of college nights spent partying with friends.

Together, these three theories—release, superiority, and surprise—explain nearly every type of humor. But you should think of them as a Venn diagram of three partially overlapping circles. Though most jokes are best explained by one theory, it is clear that many work on two levels, and some on all three. Self-deprecating humor, the easiest type to deploy, always hits on at least two. First, this type of humor allows others to feel superior at the speaker's expense. Second, audiences expect speakers to be competent and confident. Consequently, when a speaker makes a self-deprecating remark, the audience gets a delightful surprise and responds with laughter. Often that laughter is rooted in empathy, such as when Toastmasters laugh about themselves. Certain self-deprecating humor can even include the release theory too, for example when the speakers makes light of their own illness.

Tip #18: Remember to riff

The funniest winning Toastmasters speech was in 2000, when Ed Tate delivered an eye-popping 4.9 laughs per minute. He was the only prior World Champion to enter stand-up comedy's normal range of four to six laughs per minute. This is even more impressive considering the 2001 champion, Darren LaCroix, an actual stand-up comedian, garnered 3.7 laughs per minute.

With thirty-seven laughs, Ed Tate racked one up every twelve seconds. A great question to ask is: What did Ed do that Brian did not? Both drew on the full breadth of humor types, including surprise, superiority, and release. Twenty-three of Ed's laughs were principally rooted in surprise, ten in release, and four in superiority. However, Ed got laughs in clusters while Brian did not.

Telling jokes in clusters is known to comedians as riffing. The objective is to get one laugh, pause for a moment to let the laughter settle down, then elaborate with an even more outrageous or extreme comment along the same vein. Most comedians strive to apply the rule of three, moving on after three successively funnier riffs. Though it is possible to push past three, only speakers with very well-rehearsed material should attempt that in high-stakes environments.

Each one of Brian's jokes was independent. In contrast, twenty-nine of Ed's jokes were delivered in clusters of two or more. Only eight of the laughs Ed received were from stand-alone jokes. He even opened his speech with the classic comedic rule of three when he pulled a notepad and pen from his inside coat pocket, assumed an authoritative posture, and said:

There you go Mr. Tate. Next time drive a little slower. [Laughter] Speaking of slow, have you ever wondered why it takes a police officer so long to write a ticket? [Laughter] Completely eliminating all that time that you have made up. [Laughter]

The first laugh is superiority at Ed's expense for getting caught speeding. The second laugh is superiority at the officer's expense by insulting the authority figure's low sense of urgency. The third laugh is surprise due to incongruence, with a pinch of frustration release tossed in for good measure.

Though most of Ed's laugh clusters were in groups of three, he managed two four-joke sequences and even one with five! That largest group started when he dressed down a rude fellow airline passenger who was stronger and taller than Ed. The next four in this five-laugh sequence came fast and furious:

Then all of a sudden – POW! [Laughter] - his girlfriend hit him in the arm and said, "Yeah, be nice." [Laughter] Now some of you all thought I got hit, didn't you? [Laughter] He walked away in stunned silence rubbing his arm. [Laughter]

If Brian had taken his five jokes and riffed with a rule of three even once, he would have safely landed himself at an acceptable lower bound of one laugh per minute.

Tip #19: Amplify humor with vocal, physical, and facial expressiveness

Humor is one of the most difficult skills to master in public speaking. Though daunting at first glance, the easier part in the journey is crafting funny material that engages the audience in surprise, release, or superiority. However, many Toastmasters speak brilliantly funny lines and fail to get laughs. Why?

More often than not, the reason is due to a specific and easily fixed error in delivery. As if speaking in front of tens, hundreds, or thousands of eyes was not enough, the fear of telling a joke and not getting a laugh is downright terrifying. No one wants to bomb in front of friends, family, and coworkers. As a consequence, far too many speakers power through their jokes without pausing to even let the audience laugh.

As critical as silence is to capturing laughter, exaggerated vocal variety and physicality are catalysts to igniting it. Brian's "at church there was music" line demonstrated both. To deliver the line, he adopted an oratory style known to African American churchgoers as "whooping." (The "w" is silent.) This celebratory style is designed so that people feel, not just hear, a sermon. It is characterized by rhythm, frequent pauses during sentences, often accompanied by gasps, and drawn-out words at the ends of sentences. An expert in the style, the Reverend E. Dewey Smith Jr. of The Greater Travelers Rest Baptist Church, refers to it as "jazz from the pulpit." Whooping is not just vocal, it is also physical. By bending his knees, raising his arms in the air, and shaking his hands, Brian added physical emphasis to his comedy.

The third catalyst to accelerate laughter is facial expressiveness. As Brian delivered his big laugh line, "Quit!" he crossed his arms, rolled his head to the side, and took on the exaggerated frown of his malevolent academic advisor. In doing so, Brian demonstrated the critical principal that humorous facial expressiveness is simply an exaggerated version of the emotion that a character is feeling. Brian could alternatively have worn his own countenance of defeat or even led the audience in expressing the look of incredulous shock at the recommendation. It is worth noting that facial expressions alone are often enough to draw out sizable laughter.

Tip #20: All humor should further the message

To Brian Corey's credit, every one of his five jokes was original and on message. They were short, specific, and sensory. They tied either directly to music or to his personal experience. In particular, the bad advice he got from his academic advisor was especially effective in moving Brian's story forward.

Speakers are advised to avoid recycled jokes that have been passed down over time by comedians. The jokes rarely further the speaker's message, feel inauthentic, and risk falling flat if too many people have heard them before. Though telling recycled jokes is rather hard to find in the Toastmasters World Championship, Willie Jones won in 1997 despite committing this error. His core message, directed at his fellow baby boomers, was to stop regretting things you have not done and to start living. He introduced the new, but complementary, theme of not taking yourself too seriously in his conclusion and supported it with the following:

As a matter of fact, the way you should treat failure is like the preacher did when he gave his first sermon before the big preacher in the church one day. And, the sermon was really bad. And, the right reverend got up and told him, "That wasn't very good." And, he humiliated the young preacher in front of the whole audience.

And, the preacher said, "I'll do better next week."

The next week he came in and he gave a second sermon and he remembered being humiliated and he said, "I'm not going to fail this week." He said, "My fellow parishioners. I can fail, you can fail, and the Monsignor can fail. I can sin, you can sin, and the Monsignor can sin. I can to go Hell, you can go to Hell, …" You know what. Don't take yourself so seriously.

Tip #21: Pause and stay in character while the audience is laughing

Even though Brian did not deliver many laugh-inducing lines, he was well-versed in how to amplify humor with the power of the pause. In his four less funny lines, he paused for two seconds after each line. Though that may not seem like a lot, it is enough to give the audience sufficient time to start laughing. If they do not laugh much or at all, then it is also short enough to come off as a normal pause.

Brian's biggest laugh came when his academic advisor gave him the bad advice to give up his passion for music. With the audience fully engaged in laughter, he held his words for a full five seconds of silence. During the pause, Brian stayed in character as his academic advisor with his arms crossed, head turned to the side, and mouth closed in a mild scowl.

If you watch great comedians like Bill Cosby, Jerry Seinfeld, or Kathy Griffin, they generally have two modes while they wait in silence for laughter to subside. When they are playing a character, they remain in character with limited or no movement; the exception is when movement is part of the joke. When they get a laugh for something they say when they are not in character, they hold a very mild smile and either stay relatively still or move to a new stage location.

Tip #22: Bring your audience through the broadest possible emotional range

Thus far, this chapter has focused exclusively on the subject of humor, which is the most critical and most daunting tool for helping your audience experience happiness. But, happiness is just one of several human emotions.

Classifying emotion proves to be as slippery as classifying humor, if not more so. Two distinguished researchers, Paul Ekman and Robert Plutchik, have espoused overlapping but not identical theories. By studying facial microexpressions across cultures, Ekman identified six primary emotions, including: anger, disgust, fear, happiness, sadness, and surprise. Plutchik, in his visually memorable "Wheel of Emotions," posited eight paired emotions: joy-sadness; trust-disgust; fear-anger; and, surprise-anticipation.

Though either system will suit you quite well, I have found that a hybrid of the two is most effective for speech development. My "six emotions of speaking" include: anger, disgust, fear, happiness, love, and sadness. I eliminated "surprise" in Ekman's and Plutchik's models since it is so fleeting and quickly morphs into one of the other emotions as a person processes the impact of what surprised them; ditto for Plutchik's "anticipation." Lastly, I transformed Plutchik's "trust" into love because love is a more powerful and more common emotion elicited in public speaking. (The Wheel of Emotions treats love as a composite of joy and trust, but we have all seen love exist without either.)

Most winning Toastmasters speeches manage to hit every one of those emotions in just five to seven minutes. That takes incredibly careful writing. Let's see how Brian Corey did by identifying at least one instance of each emotion:

- Anger: "I thought about being in the car with my brother, arguing over what song was going to be played on the radio."

- Disgust: "The message [my academic advisor] gave me was life changing. I can sum it up in one word: 'Quit!'"
- Fear: *(not present)*
- Happiness: "Music has a way to move the spirit, ease the mind and uplift the soul."
- Love: *(not present)*
- Sadness: "There I was, a musician. I played the music that moved the soul, eased the mind, and uplifted the spirit. But, there was no one to uplift my spirit."

Brian's speech is extremely rich in the emotions of happiness and sadness. You have to stretch a bit to detect anger and disgust. Listening to his speech, I got the sense that Brian truly enjoys music; it makes him happy. Though I have no doubt that music is a passion for him, he did not quite express that passion as love in his speech. Similarly, he had a golden opportunity to allow the audience to experience fear if he had more explicitly stated that he was close to failing out of school and facing angry parents and an uncertain future.

Next, consider Ed Tate's speech:

- Anger: "Now I was upset with United. It was because of their policy that I was going to miss my flight."
- Disgust: "I'm a frequent flyer with United. I've paid tens of thousands of dollars with this airline."
- Fear: "I started to walk towards them. By the way, did I mention that he was tall? Six foot four, about 220.

Folks, don't let the video screens fool you, I am not a big man."

- Happiness: "Her fingers danced across the keyboard and she presented me with a ticket on the 2:00 flight to Phoenix. Hallelujah, hallelujah!"
- Love: "I made eye contact with the customer service agent and all of a sudden it occurred to me that she was trying to do the best that she could. She was trying to provide for her family just like me."
- Sadness: "There was no way I was going to make my noon flight. It's going to be one of those days."

Like Ed, most former champions clearly checked the box on all six emotions. However, some did not. This meant that Brian Corey still had a fighting chance of winning.

Tip #23: Express your emotions, but don't lose control

If a speaker is not able to express his or her own emotions, then the audience will never be able to experience them during his speech. The good news is that every speaker who makes it to the stage in the finals of the World Championship of Public Speaking is able to get emotionally worked up in front of an audience.

Many less-practiced speakers struggle with too little emotional disclosure for a number of reasons. The most common is nervousness. When you are nervous, you lose expressiveness in your face and your voice. You restrain your physical-range movement.

Even when the nervousness subsides, some speakers fear that showing emotion exposes their egos. That is true. But so what? The price you pay for encasing your ego in a three-foot-thick wall of concrete is that you fail to connect with your audience. That is too dear a price to pay in any setting.

With a relatively narrow emotional range, Brian Corey was in no risk of losing control. However, there were several of Brian's competitors who approached the line, but we have not met them yet. Fortunately, a number of past World Champions serve as good examples, but none more so than David Henderson. David spoke through tears for most of his speech as he relived the tragic loss of his childhood friend.

Of the six emotions of speaking, four actually allow you to talk more—anger, disgust, happiness, and love. In contrast, fear and sadness make you clam up. It is pretty hard to get overwhelmed by the fear that you relive when telling a story. Hence, the only emotion that typically poses a risk for speakers is sadness.

Watching a Toastmasters contest can sometimes be a bit like watching a Shakespearean tragedy; there are countless stories of losing loved ones to incurable illness, accident, or simply old age. Four of the nine contestants in the 2012 contest mentioned either death or serious illness. However, sob stories rarely win—only four of the past seventeen champions played the tragedy card.

Keep The Music Alive

Central message(s)	Perseverance
Duration	7.2 Minutes
Words per minute	100
Laughs per minute	0.70

Table 4.1: Vital statistics for *Keep The Music Alive* by Brian Corey

(Introduction)

Ba dum bap, ba dum bap, ba dum bap, ba dum bap. Ba dum ba dum ba do bap, ba dum bap, ba dum bap.

Music has a way to move the spirit, ease the mind and uplift the soul. Even in a room with 3,000 Toastmasters.

Contest Chair, fellow Toastmasters and guests, music has always been a part of my life. As a child, at home, there was music. In the car, there was music. At church, there was music.

(Part 1)

I enjoyed music so much that in middle school and high school I participated in the band program. I remember receiving my trumpet for the first time. After high school, there was no doubt in my mind that I was going to major in music education.

(Part 2)

In college, the demands on a music major were great. I would often look at my classmates and they seemed to have plenty of time to study and party. But me? All my time was spent practicing, rehearsing, studying, and in class.

I was at a moment in my life where I needed some encouragement. What better place to go than my academic advisor. I knew he would fold his arms, lean back in his chair and say, 'Son, we've all been there. Stick with this. You can do it.'

Boy, was I wrong. The message he gave me was life changing. I can sum it up in one word: 'Quit!'

As I made my way back to the car, I began to think about all the time I had invested in music. I thought about high school, how I anticipated the band competitions. I thought about middle school, and my father bringing the trumpet home, the excitement on my face.

I thought about being in the car with my brother, arguing over what song was going to be played on the radio. I thought about the words from my academic advisor. There I was, a musician. I played the music that moved the soul, eased the mind, and uplifted the spirit. But, there was no one to uplift my spirit.

I started the car, turned on the radio. There was this beat. I seemed to forget about everything that I was going through. It was Yolanda Adams singing 'Never give up.' The song says 'Keep your dream alive, don't let it die. There's something deep inside that's inspiring you to try. Don't stop, never give up. Never give up on you. Don't give up.' At that moment, with that message, I decided to persevere.

(Part 3)

May 2007, I graduated from East Carolina University, located in Greenville, North Carolina, with a degree in music education. It wasn't until I stepped into the classroom that I began to understand why you should never give up on your dream.

If I had given up, I would have never had the opportunity to meet Joe. Joe was 16, he was one of my band students. Aside from working with music, I was to work with him on his math and reading. There were times that Joe wanted to give up, but I said 'Joe, you can never give up, as long as I'm around.'

I can't begin to tell you the excitement on my face when Joe came up to me and said, "Hey, Mr. Corey, guess what?"

"What Joe?"

"I made a 100 on my math exam!"

"Good job, Joe. You can do it."

The most exciting thing was when I learned that Joe, who was 16 in the eighth grade, had scored a B on his math and reading EOGs, which in North Carolina is the end of grade test. I was glad I never gave up.

(Conclusion)

Ladies and gentlemen, you should not give up on your dreams either, because you have something this world needs. There is something inside that only you can provide. Just like Mozart, Beethoven, Michael Jackson gave us music, you have something extraordinary.

The next time you feel like quitting and giving up. Understand. It's not about us. It's about Joe. It's about the people we touch. The lives we change. When we never give up and encourage others to do the same, we can keep the music alive.

Ba dum bap, ba dum bap, ba dum bap, ba dum bap. Contest Chair.

CHAPTER 5: Language

Tip #24: Use the smallest and simplest possible words to express your message

The fifth slot brought forth the day's first and only female speaker. "Diane Parker. Yet, Here I Stand. Yet, Here I Stand. Diane Parker."

The funeral scene that Diane set with her speech was dark. But she did not deliver a memorial service for a person. She held a memorial service to vanquish her painful past memories. By releasing her own baggage and inviting her audience to do the same, she expressed her core theme—the power of mindfulness.

If you go to a Toastmasters club anywhere in the world tonight, you will likely be encouraged to use the word of the day. More often than not, it is a "ten-dollar word" like quixotic, sanguine, or mellifluous. It is a fun game that encourages quick thinking on the part of each speaker and active listening on the part of the audience. Also, there is a 100 percent guarantee of laughter when a speaker uses the word.

The problem with the word-of-the-day concept is that it perpetuates the myth that great speakers need to use their extensive vocabularies. A speaker's job is to connect emotionally with the listeners in his or her audience and hopefully inspire them to look at the world differently. A speaker's job is never to impress an audience with vocabulary (or anything else for that matter). If a speaker taxes the audience's cognitive processing ability, then he or she will fail to connect.

Consider the following sentence: "Please convene with me for an exiguous quantity of seconds of laconism in the reminiscence of the quietus of someone very dear to me." That sentence is written at the reading level of a college freshman, who would probably still have to look up a couple of the words to make sense of it.

Speeches are written for the ear and not for the eye. Here is that same sentence as Diane Parker expressed it in the opening of her speech: "Please join me in a few seconds of silence in the memory of the passing of someone very dear to me." Though her speech had mature themes, Diane crafted her speech to be readable by a fourth grader and therefore accessible to everyone from nine to ninety.

Devised by Rudolf Flesch and developed by J. Peter Kincaid, the Flesch-Kincaid Grade Level (F-K) algorithm was first used in 1978 to measure the difficulty of technical manuals used by the US military. Today, it forms the basis of the readability statistics in Microsoft Word.

As it turns out, Diane was right on target with using the smallest and simplest possible words to express her message. Using the F-K measurement, winning speeches over the preceding seventeen years ranged at grade levels between 3.5 and 7.7. At 4.3, Diane was just shy of the average of 5.8 but not remarkably so.

The 2011 champion, Jock Elliott, is widely acknowledged as being an artist with words. His speech, titled "Just So Lucky," stressed the importance of loving your family, friends, and partners. Read the following passage with your best Australian mental accent to glimpse his mastery:

First, over here, the friends of my blood. That is my family. My mom and dad, my brothers and sisters, my children. This is an old friendship forged from birth. A lifelong link between my past and my future. Of course, we have had our differences, just like every family. But, I am just so lucky because we got over those. And anyway, if you cannot shout at your brother and sister, who can you shout at? And blood is thicker than water. And no one is thicker than my brother.

Jock's words are simple and his sentences are short. And yet, the listeners not only visualize Jock's experience but also are transported into the emotional world of their past family interactions. This brief passage is rife with anger and forgiveness, with love, and even with humor.

Speaking at nearly an eighth-grade level, Dwayne Smith shared how music can provide life-saving hope in his 2002 speech, "Music in the Key of Life." Here is a passage from his winning speech:

One of my favorite styles of music is called bebop. It's a genre of modern jazz that has severely revamped chord structures, unusually accented rhythmic phrasing and lots of improvisation.

Many of us live our lives in a bebop kind of way in that we tend to do things differently from others. We take on life as it comes and we make up stuff as we go along. Now you may have figured out that beboppers don't like to plan. In fact, they like to do as the great jazz singer, Ella Fitzgerald, once said and I quote, "They just want to live, baby." They don't want to plan.

Contrary to what you might assume, the F-K score is not based on a dictionary. It does not know that "genre," "chord structures," and "improvisation" are more complex than "type," "harmony," and "creativity." The grade level goes up for two simple reasons. The first reason it increases is due to long sentences. The second is when the text contains a large amount of multisyllabic words. Jock's speech averaged 10.8 words per sentence and had a scant 4 percent of words with three or more syllables. Though Mr. Smith had the same percentage of long words, he averaged nearly double the sentence length at 20.7. Just remember, listeners like short sentences, punctuated by pauses.

Tip #25: Intensify your language with vivid images and sensory detail

Using language that is simple does not mean that you need to compromise on its intensity. Diane used simple language to convey powerful emotion in the following line: "Even though she caused me enormous grief and daily strife, may she forever rest in peace and keep the hell out of my life."

In his outstanding book *The Presentation Secrets of Steve Jobs*, Carmine Gallo describes the technology pioneer's language as simple, concrete, and emotional. The key to building emotional intensity is the use of descriptive adjectives and adverbs. For Steve Jobs, that included words like "amazing," "incredible," and "unbelievable." Diane embraced this concept with her use of superlatives in "enormous grief and daily strife."

Tip #26: Encapsulate your core message in a catchphrase and drill it in

Though there may be rare times when speakers should let their core message subtly sink in, the Toastmasters International Speech Contest is not one of them. The question is not whether to have a catchphrase; the question is how to construct and deliver it.

Andrew Kneebone, the first speaker of the day, meant to have one but buried it in his conclusion and only used it once. When I spoke to Andrew, he revealed that he built his speech around a single kernel of wisdom that his father imprinted in him—"His blood is your blood." Short and rhythmic, this expression does have two key characteristics of a powerful catchphrase. However, the listener has to think in order to relate those words to Andrew's core themes of perseverance and respect.

The second speaker, Stuart Pink, used his catchphrase—"Brain Lifting"—a total of eight times. He followed the best practice of using it at least once in his introduction, body, and conclusion.

It is kinesthetic. Moreover, he used it as his title as many past champions have done.

With "turn disaster into laughter," Ronald Melvin crafted a catchphrase that is about as textbook-perfect as they come. Like Andrew Kneebone's, it is short and rhythmic. Like Stuart Pink, Ronald used it as his title and reinforced the message in each part of his speech. But, he did something that his two predecessors did not. He made it action-centric to the point where everybody in the room could take it with them and apply it when they left.

Brian Corey, the speaker following Ronald, took an approach similar to Andrew Kneebone's. He delivered his catchphrase only in his conclusion, when he repeated his title "keep the music alive." Again the listener needs to do a considerable amount of thinking to remember that keeping the music alive is a metaphor for persevering when the going gets tough. The following play on an old adage, though borderline cliché, might have worked better as a catchphrase: "When the going gets tough, the tough keep going."

That brings us to our present speaker, Diane, who used the catchphrase "Yet, here I stand." There is a lot to like about her catchphrase. It is short. It is visual. Though it did not appear in her introduction, she used it five times, then cleverly morphed it into "Yet, I still stand." Purists might argue that the transformation was a tactical error, but on deep consideration, I do believe it makes her speech more powerful. Her catchphrase does not require cognitive horsepower to get the core message that we serve ourselves better when we release the pain of the past and instead focus on the power of the present. If it has one flaw in construction, it is that the audience would need to use the phrase as an affirmation rather than an action prompter.

Between 1995 and 2011, twelve of the seventeen speakers had clearly distinguishable catchphrases. Eight of those twelve used their speech title as their catchphrase. Making this choice has three huge benefits. First, by using your catchphrase as your title, you force yourself to stay on message. It makes the spine of your speech unambiguously clear so that you can edit thoughtfully. Second, and more importantly, following this approach makes your core message unambiguously clear to your audience. Finally, if you are in a competitive speaking environment, the judges need only look at your title to recall the power of your speech.

If you ask prior World Champions which catchphrase stands out in their minds as the best ever, then nearly every one of them will point to Lance Miller's in 2005. His catchphrase—"The Ultimate Question"—is not his title. It was not even the question itself that he revealed in his very first sentence:

"The ultimate question, that question that has plagued man since the dawn of time and that question that each and every one of us must ask at some point in our life, do you validate?"

Lance delivers his catchphrase when an office receptionist validates his parking ticket:

She took her little machine and she went cha-ching and as she handed it back, she looked at me and she said, "There's something special about you." I took the ticket and headed for the elevator, but I stopped and turned around and just said, "Thank you."

In total, Mr. Miller used "cha-ching" thirteen times. At one point, he even repeated it three times in a row. He closed with the following words:

Do you validate? But, this is not what's important. What's important is can you cha-ching? Can you cha-ching? Can you cha-ching? [PAUSE] You've been a great audience.

Lance Miller's catchphrase is not even a word. It is a sound. But more importantly, it is a powerful metaphor for what people need to do, simply to compliment others, to make the world a better place. Short. Rhythmic. Crystal clear. Repeated. Actionable. And, in just one more word... perfect.

Tip #27: Use a callback to elegantly link your conclusion to your introduction

The vast majority of speakers use callbacks in their speeches either for humorous or for dramatic effect. Callbacks, or loops, are repetitions of words or phrases from a prior part of the speech. Most often, callbacks tie together the speaker's introduction and his or her conclusion. With humor, the speaker gives the audience a feeling of being "in on the joke." With drama, the speaker instantly conjures the emotions felt in the earlier part of the speech.

Though catchphrases are the most frequent applications of callbacks, callbacks can have even more impact when applied to other words or phrases. In her introduction, Diane sang a secular modification of the spiritual "Oh Happy Day": "Oh happy day, oh happy day. When I buried all of my past away." She closed the loop by singing the same phrase at the end of her speech.

Callbacks need not be delivered word for word. For instance, former champion Mark Brown started his speech with, "You never get a second chance to make a first impression." He ended with, "Because everyone deserves a second chance." This was a particularly clever juxtaposition of two contradictory pieces of conventional wisdom.

While Diane and Mr. Brown used verbatim references, callbacks work even when they are rather indirect. The 1996 winner, David Nottage, told a story in his introduction about struggling to learn how to ride a bicycle when he was six years old. Then, in the body of his speech, he illustrated the importance of perseverance in the face of failure. He shared another personal story about failing in a business he started. In addition, he referenced South African civil rights leader Nelson Mandela and Olympic gymnast Kerri Strug. (After straining her left ankle on her first vault, Strug secured a gold medal for her team by courageously landing her second vault on her right foot.) Mr. Nottage ended his speech with a callback to his opening story:

She [Strug] had every right to stay down, but she got up.
Mary Pickford said it best when she said, "This thing that we
call failure. This thing that we call failure... It's not the falling
down, it's the staying down." Ladies and gentlemen, how easy,
how easy is it for us, you and I, to remember this simple secret
for success? It should be as easy as falling off a bike.

As a final example, consider the approach that the 1997 champion, Willie Jones, used. During his speech, he described helping his friends fix their computers by instructing them on how to reboot. He ended the first part of his speech with, "I can hear this sound that goes 'Boing!' and that lets me know that everything is fine. That sound is 'Boing!' Remember that." He closes the loop with his final words by repeating the sound: "Just because you grow up, doesn't mean you have to grow old. Those of you who are baby boomers, let me hear you go, 'Boing!'"

Tip #28: Use figurative language to personify your opponent

The primary opponent in nearly every Toastmasters speech is a concept rather than a person. Typically, it is the foil to the speaker's core message. The opponent to love is hate; to tolerance, discrimination; to perseverance, quitting. Though it is perfectly fine to keep your opponent as a concept, many competitors have decided to personify the evil.

For the first few moments of Diane Parker's speech, the audience really believes that she was going to reminisce about a lost friend. But she soon reveals that her friend, with her through thick and thin, was actually her difficult past. Diane Parker not only animated her intangible opponent, she gave it a funeral, complete with an opening prayer, a scripture reading, and a eulogy.

Diane Parker used an approach very similar to the 2010 runner-up, Robert MacKenzie. Mr. MacKenzie personified his alter ego, going so far as to give him the name "Bobby Backwards." Bobby was the voice inside Robert's head that was holding him back. He was the voice of fear that said "no" to change. Cleverly, Robert gave Bobby his own place on the stage. Bobby was a giant—eight feet in diameter and stretched from the floor to the ceiling. He was so big that Mr. MacKenzie actually stepped inside his alter ego:

Now the amazing feature of my alter ego is, because he is so big, there is a dark space inside with a door. I can actually open this door and when I step inside, and close the door, nobody [mouths words silently for five seconds] hears anything that anybody else is saying either.

In many circles, personifying your opponent is considered to be a trite technique and should therefore be used sparingly. The first time an audience member sees personification used in this way, it seems very novel; the second time, not so much. In the span between 1995 and 2011, only one champion did so. Mark Brown, in 1995, personified intolerance, indifference, and ignorance as a beast.

Tip #29: Polish your speech with rhetorical wordplay

There is a vast array of rhetorical devices that you can use to enhance your speech. Though some have unfamiliar names, you will recognize most of them from the examples provided. Here is a list of the more common types found in modern public speaking:

- Assonance and Consonance: These kissing cousins refer to the repetition of the same sound two or more times in rapid succession. Assonance is the repetition of vowel sounds; consonance is the repetition of consonant sounds. Diane Parker used consonance with "seconds of silence" and with "closest companion and confidant." In addition, she blended assonance and consonance in "weeping and wailing, fanning and fainting."

- Anaphora, Epistrophe, and Symploce: Anaphora is the repetition of the same word or words at the beginning of successive phrases or sentences. Epistrophe is the same concept applied to the ends of phrases or sentences. Symploce combines the two. In the following passage, Diane used anaphora in the first sentence by repeating the word "every." Then, in the second sentence, she uses symploce by repeating "never" at the beginning and "me" at the end: "She's been in sync with every move I made, every step I took. She's never questioned me, and never doubted me."

- Anadiplosis: This is the repetition of the last word of one sentence at or near the beginning of the next. Though

Diane Parker did not use this rhetorical device, Ed Tate provides a good example: "...on this particular occasion, in addition to [the gate agent], there was a man in a suit. Usually suits mean trouble..."

- Hendiatris: This is the use of three words in succession to express a single concept. Ronald Melvin used hendiatris to describe a wedding celebration: "I went to the reception just in time to see two young ladies walking in the door. Wine, women, and song."

In addition to these fancier rhetorical techniques, good old repetition of phrases or sentences is a powerful way to underscore key messages.

Tip #30: Apply the rule of three in lists of similar items

In 1956, Princeton psychologist George A. Miller published a groundbreaking article entitled: "The Magical Number Seven, Plus or Minus Two: Some Limits on Our Capacity for Processing Information." In it, he summarized experiments that tested how accurately people were able to first absorb and then communicate different amounts of information. He cited prior research that explored four of the five senses: hearing (pitch and loudness); taste (saltiness and sweetness); sight (spatial position of objects); touch (intensity, duration, and locations of vibrations on the skin). He ended his somewhat impenetrable article with the following, more accessible, warning against overinterpreting the research:

And finally, what about the magical number seven? What about the seven wonders of the world, the seven seas, the seven deadly sins, the seven daughters of Atlas in the Pleiades, the seven ages of man, the seven levels of hell, the seven primary colors, the seven notes of the musical scale, and the seven days of the week? What about the seven-point rating scale, the seven categories for absolute judgment, the seven objects in the span of attention, and the seven digits in the span of immediate memory? For the present I propose to withhold judgment. Perhaps there is something deep and profound behind all these sevens, something just calling out for us to discover it. But I suspect that it is only a pernicious, Pythagorean coincidence.

Over the years, many academics have tested the validity of what has come to be known as Miller's Law—the idea that people can hold seven, plus or minus two, items in their working memory. Though the magical number seven remains embedded in conventional wisdom, scientists agree that there is no single magic number. The number of items we are able to remember depends on the size of each information chunk, the relationship between the chunks, and our individual cognitive ability.

However, with the advent of modern brain imaging, three scholars rose to Miller's challenge to discover if there really is a magic number. Jennifer J. Summerfield, Demis Hassabis, and

Eleanor A. Maguire asked nineteen people to construct imaginary scenes in their minds as they listened to groups of short phrases. Each phrase contained a descriptor and a noun. For example, one group of three phrases was "a dark blue carpet," "a carved chest of drawers," and "an orange striped pencil." They tested groups of three to six elements while they watched the brain activity of the subjects using fMRI technology. In addition, they asked the people to indicate on a keypad how difficult they found the trial, the vividness of the imagined scene, and the perceived degree of integration between the elements.

The researchers made two important discoveries. First, brain activity steadily increases in the core locations of the brain up to and including the addition of a third element. Then, activity suddenly stabilized. Second, subjects rated the tests with three elements as easiest to visualize, most vivid, and most integrated.

By now, you are probably wondering what all this has to do with public speaking. The types of lists Summerfield, Hassabis, and Maguire studied are exactly the kinds of lists that speakers use. There is something satisfying and symmetrical about the rule of three.

Brian Corey, the prior speaker, embraced this concept throughout his speech. In his introduction, he revealed that music permeated every part of his life: "As a child, at home, there was music. In the car, there was music. At church, there was music." In the body of his speech, he shared: "I played the music that moved the soul, eased the mind, and uplifted the spirit." A triplet also appears in his conclusion: "Just like Mozart, Beethoven, [and] Michael Jackson gave us music, you have something extraordinary [inside]."

For the most part, Diane Parker demonstrated a preference for pairs. Often used for contrast, pairs are punchy. In fact, starting with "thick and thin," she strung four of them together artfully in her introduction:

We are gathered here today for the home going celebration of someone who has been close to me for years, been by my side through thick and thin. She's been my closest companion and confidant. She's been in sync with every move I made, every step I took. She's never questioned me, and never doubted me.

Though she had plenty of groups of two elements and even one series of six, she did not apply the rule of three until her conclusion. There, she used it twice with, "Shakespeare wrote many great tragedies of life, Romeo and Juliet, Othello and Hamlet" and with "Earth to earth, ashes to ashes, dust to dust."

Diane's disproportionate use of pairs had the overall effect of making her speech sound staccato and overly intense. Groups of three typically highlight similar elements. Had she used a few more, Diane would have added a soothing and contemplative effect that would have balanced her speech.

The rule of three is of course just a rule of thumb. Single items are especially definitive and powerful. As mentioned, pairs highlight contrast and threes emphasize similarity. However, there are times when very long lists are appropriate. Consider the following portion of Craig Valentine's winning speech:

But you've turned your back on it [your spirit] and you wonder why you have your ups and downs and goods and bads and backs and forths and bottoms and tops and ins and outs... and the bottom line is you've turned your back on your spirit and that's why you stumble and why you fall.

Craig's verbally acrobatic list, delivered very rapidly, builds intensity to a boiling point. Then, following a dramatic pause and a slow rehashing of what he said, he provides the cure:

Silence, that's it. Silence, you're trying to tell me that I never take the time to just be silent and still and listen to my spirit.

Tip #31: Avoid quoting famous people

One of the persistent myths among Toastmasters around the world is that talented speakers must be able to sling famous quotations at the drop of a hat. However, that belief is sorely misguided. In almost all circumstances, using famous quotes is unoriginal and cliché. Rattling off quotes is most damaging because the practice is inauthentic. Audiences want to hear you, to listen to your stories. If they want to read quotes, then they can pick up a copy of *Bartlett's Familiar Quotations*.

During the 2012 contest, Diane Parker and four additional speakers used quotations during their speeches. Since Diane synthesized a funeral for her past, she used biblical and other religious passages in the introduction, body, and conclusion of her speech.

At lower levels of the contest, speakers frequently open or close with a quote. A couple of finalists even did this during the 2012 competition. Kenny Ray Morgan, whom we will meet a bit later, used the overly formulaic technique of opening and closing with the same quote: "Do that which you fear most, and the death of fear is certain." This quote belongs to Mark Twain.

The principle that quotes are bad is not just a matter of personal opinion. Among the seventeen winning speeches between 1995 and 2011, speakers used canned quotations only four times. And that is with a very loose definition of what constitutes a "famous" source. In 1995, Mark Brown opened with, "You never get a second chance to make a first impression," a quote of unknown attribution. In 2003, Jim Key quoted Martin Luther King in the body of his speech. The 2009 winner, Mark Hunter, referenced Deepak Chopra, also in the body of his speech.

If there is one exception to the "no quotations" rule, it is found in the introduction of Jock Elliott's 2011 winning speech, which starts: "John Lau says in his Facebook page that 'Everyone has a best friend at each stage of their life. Only a lucky few have the same one.'" This quote works for two reasons. The first is novelty; it is unlikely that anyone in the audience had ever heard it before. The second is that it customized his speech, one that he had polished many, many times over the course of several years, for that audience on that day. Who is John Lau? He was the emcee of the contest on the day Jock won!

Tip #32: Surprise your audience with misdirection

If there is a second exception to the "no quotations" rule, then it is to be found in Jim Key's 2003 speech. The overarching message of Jim's speech is that it is never too late to follow your dreams. He uses the word dream twenty-four times in his speech.

After he had already used the word "dream" nine times, Jim proceeded: "Ladies and gentlemen, we were meant to dream. We were meant to dream. Dr. Martin Luther King, Jr., one of the greatest dreamers of our age, said..." At this point, everybody in the audience was expecting Jim to say: "I have a dream!" Instead, he used another quotation that surprised the audience:

"The time is always right to do what is right," and that means that if it was right for us to dream as children then it's just as right for us to dream as adults.

Like Jock's quote, Jim's quote shares a sense of novelty because few, if any, in the audience were familiar with it. It comes from a lesser known speech that Dr. King delivered at Oberlin College in October 1964. Of course, the other reason this quote works is because of misdirection. One of the great principles of public speaking is that your audience should never be able to finish your sentence. Misdirection takes this one clever step further.

Tip #33: The larger the audience, the shorter the speech

When Sean Shannon delivered Hamlet's 260-word soliloquy "To be or not to be" in 23.8 seconds in August 1995, he became the world's fastest talker at 655 words per minute. Though an amazing curiosity, his performance lacked the emotional intensity of Sir Laurence Olivier's 1948 cinematic masterpiece. Mr. Olivier delivered the same passage in three minutes and eighteen seconds, or seventy-nine words per minute.

In the Toastmasters World Championship, speakers must deliver their speech within five to seven minutes, with a thirty-second buffer on either side. Contestants see a green light at five minutes followed by a yellow light at six minutes. The red light comes on at seven minutes and stays on; there is no indication provided if the disqualifying threshold of seven minutes and thirty seconds is breached.

Though none of the speakers went over time in the 2012 contest, many speakers have had victory stolen from their grasp in prior years. This happens mainly because speakers fail to adequately account for audience reaction time, particularly for the delay added by laughter. At each level of the contest, as the audience size increases, speakers must trim words.

In her speech, Diane Parker filled seven minutes and twelve seconds speaking at a rate of ninety-two words per minute. If she had just thirty-five more words in her speech, she would have been disqualified. That is fewer words than are in this paragraph!

Over the past seventeen years, the average champion delivered 892 words in seven minutes and fifteen seconds. That works out to just under 125 words per minute.

Your rate of speech may vary greatly from the average. The fastest champion in recent history was Craig Valentine, at 198 words per minute. His call to action was that everybody should take five minutes of contemplative silence each day. To build tension for the extended moments of silence in his speech, he delivered artful bursts of words. However, he knew that his audience would not fully comprehend what he was saying. So, after each burst, he slowed down and repeated his message.

Vikas Jhingran and Brett Rutledge were at the low end of the range, speaking at a rate of ninety-eight and ninety-nine words per minute, respectively. At ninety-two words per minute, the lowest by far of all the contestants, Diane Parker may have spoken a little too slowly.

Yet Here I Stand

Central message(s)	Mindfulness
Duration	7.2 Minutes
Words per minute	92
Laughs per minute	0.84

Table 5.1: Vital statistics for *Yet, Here I Stand* by Diane Parker

(Introduction)

Contest Chair, my fellow Toastmasters and guests. Please join me in a few seconds of silence in the memory of the passing of someone very dear to me. Thank you.

We are gathered here today for the home going celebration of someone who has been close to me for years, been by my side through thick and thin. She's been my closest companion and confidant. She's been in sync with every move I made, every step I took. She's never questioned me and never doubted me.

Her name is... my past! Now typically at most funerals, there's a lot of weeping and wailing, fanning and fainting. But at this funeral, there will be none of that. In fact, we're going to sing with great jubilation. 'Oh happy day, oh happy day. When I buried all of my past away.' Then we will shout. Let me hear you say hey, hey, hey, hey.

[Audience: Hey, hey, hey, hey.]

Hey, hey, hey, hey.

[Audience: Hey, hey, hey, hey.]

Hey, I might even do a bit of break dancing, since I'm afraid I might truly break something and we'll go to a funeral for real. That just won't work.

(Part 1)

Let us begin the service with a humble prayer. Thank you for setting me free from my past. I commend her life into your very capable hands. Even though she caused me enormous grief and daily strife, may she forever rest in peace and keep the hell out of my life. Can I get an amen?

(Part 2)

Let's move on to the selected scripture reading. Yea, though I walk through the valley of the shadow of death, I will fear not my past, because you are with me and you will take that rod and spank her apple-shaped behind, which will greatly comfort me. Amen.

(Part 3)

Let's move on to the eulogy. Ladies and gentlemen, we all have things from our past that we'd rather not reveal. Situations and experiences that cause us to hang our heads in shame and sorrow. We'd rather wear a mask, living our lives as if we are attending a masquerade ball, to hide the pain from our past. It's time to drop the mask and deal with your past. Here are some insights into my past.

My family was riddled with drugs and alcohol abuse. Yet, here I stand. My nephew was murdered because he refused to join a gang. Yet here I stand. My father died of prostate cancer and diabetes, yet here I stand. My best friend gave birth to a beautiful baby boy. I later discovered the father was my fiancé. Yet, here I stand. My car was totaled and I had back injuries and was told I would never recover. But here I stand. Violated at the tender age of 16, yet here I still stand.

Stop traveling down the highway of your past. Yesterday is gone, tomorrow is not promised. Maximize this day. You have to look at your past and say 'Past, it's your turn to lie in the coffin. You will no longer cling dearly to my life. In fact, I pronounce you DOA. Dead on arrival.'

(Conclusion)

Shakespeare wrote many great tragedies of life, Romeo and Juliet, Othello and Hamlet. The greatest tragedy in life is not death, but living your life bound by traumatic experiences from your past. I will no longer reap what my past continues to sow.

If you ever felt you've been held back because of your past, organize a funeral. Invite your family and friends, write the obituary, deliver the eulogy, then close the casket and say, 'In spite of my past, here I still stand.' The power of the past is dead and anything dead ought to be buried. Earth to earth, ashes to ashes, dust to dust.

As we depart for the burial service, let us exit with joy in our hearts, singing 'Oh happy day, oh happy day. When I buried all of my past away.' Contest Chair.

CHAPTER 6:
Verbal Delivery

Tip #34: Exploit the many-faceted power of the pause

"Our sixth contestant is Palaniappa Subramaniam. Finding the Right Shoes. Finding the Right Shoes. Palaniappa Subramaniam." When Palaniappa walked onto the stage, most of the people in the audience did not notice that he was wearing a sneaker on his right foot and a dress shoe on his left. He delivered the introduction of his speech as follows:

[3 second opening pause] Mahatma Gandhi once said [pause], "If all [pause] enemies were to step into the shoes of their adversaries [pause], all of the misunderstandings and misadventures in the world [pause] would be solved [pause]." So, I decided to step into my wife's high heeled shoes [pause for laughter], and the only thing I understood was the pain. [pause for laughter]

Contest Chair, fellow judges, ladies and gentlemen [pause]. Shoes [pause]. They come in many shapes, many sizes [pause for laughter]. Some [pause] are designed to run [pause], some are designed to walk [pause]. But at the end of the day [pause], what is their [pause] sole purpose [pause for laughter]? Not this sole [pause for laughter while raising right foot].

It is to carry you [pause] to your destination [pause] in life [pause]. Therefore [pause], finding the right shoe [pause] should not be [pause] a trivial pursuit [pause]. When I got up this morning [pause], I couldn't decide [pause]. I read the dress code, it said semi [pause to raise foot] formal [pause for laughter while raising left foot]. So, I came prepared [pause for laughter].

But, the important question is, why do we often feel [pause] that another man's shoes [pause] are so much more easier [sic] to walk in [pause], and we always want to be in his shoes [pause]? We lose focus [pause] on our own shoe [pause] that is already here [pause].

Great speakers like Palaniappa know that silence is the single most effective vocal technique available. In his ninety-second introduction, Palaniappa paused thirty eight times. That works out to one pause every two and a half seconds. And yet, his delivery was in no way stilted, quite the opposite in fact. His pauses gave his audience time to savor his message.

Pauses serve four critical purposes and have a fifth special benefit. The first purpose, to add dramatic effect, is why Palaniappa paused for three seconds after planting his feet at center stage. His silence matched the average for prior Toastmasters World Champions, though some started with zero delay and one, Jim Key in 2003, waited eleven seconds. A portion of the pause allows supporters to finish clapping. However, speakers use the sheer silence to begin developing a deep connection with the audience.

They make eye contact with a person or a group of people for a second on the left-hand side. Then, they do the same on the right before centering their gaze. Humans are hardwired to increase their attention during silence, and seasoned presenters take every advantage of their audience's evolutionary defense mechanism. The dramatic pause is most often used at the opening of a speech, but it can be used before, during, and, more often, after a significant point. That is precisely why Palaniappa's opening quote was chockablock with pauses.

The second purpose of the pause is to allow the audience time to process what the speaker is saying. I refer to this as the comprehension pause. Speakers typically pause for one beat, the time it takes to vocalize one short music note, at commas, and for two beats at periods. As such, comprehension pauses should be thought of as verbal punctuation marks.

The third purpose of silence was introduced in the chapter on humor. With six instances in his introduction, Palaniappa demonstrated mastery of the humorous pause. Among those pauses, the most artful was when he remained quiet after saying, "Shoes. They come in many shapes, many sizes." At that moment, the majority of his audience noticed his mismatched shoes and let out a resounding laugh.

At the end of Palaniappa's introduction, he paused again to signal the transition into the body of his speech. This fourth purpose, the transitional pause, is typically longer and allows the speaker to move to a new location on the stage if desired. In Palaniappa's case, he paused for a full three seconds before winding the clock back to when he was ten years old.

I mentioned that the pause has a fifth, special benefit. Filler words such as "um," "ah," "like," and "you know" have infected everyday conversational speech. When people get on stage, they get nervous. The more nervous they get, the more filler words they utter. Getting comfortable with silence is the only way to cure filler words. To gain that comfort, practice the comprehension pause by staying quiet at natural breaks in phrases and sentences.

The majority of Toastmasters World Champions draft their speeches verbatim. For the most part, they indicate only dramatic pauses in their text because the other four types of pauses are second nature and would otherwise add too much clutter.

Among prior world champions, Ed Tate is broadly acknowledged as the foremost master of the dramatic pause. There are two instances in his 2000 speech that are envied by speakers on the competitive circuit. The first was his introductory pause. He began with a four-second pause during which he made eye contact with the vast majority of the audience. At that point, through another nine seconds of silence, he authoritatively stiffened his posture and reached into his inside coat pocket to write himself a speeding ticket.

As an interesting side note, Ed's opening silence actually saved him from disqualification. During the contest, speakers can talk for as little as four minutes and thirty seconds or as long as seven minutes and thirty seconds. The official rule book states: "Timing will begin with the contestant's first definite verbal or nonverbal communication with the audience. This usually will be the first word uttered by the contestant, but would include any other communication such as sound effects, a staged act by another person, etc." By the letter of the law, Ed's speech began when he lifted his arm to reach into his coat pocket. Timed precisely, his speech was seven minutes and thirty-six seconds. Since at least one of the timekeepers was slow with his or her trigger finger and there is no instant replay, he was saved.

Ed's second noteworthy dramatic pause came about a third of the way into his speech. There comes a point in his story where he is describing how a young man, accompanied by his girlfriend, is standing in line and arguing with a United Airlines ticketing representative about his missed flight:

The customer agent said, "Sir [pause], the next flight where I can get both of you on the flight is at 6:00 [pause]." He said, "Do the math, lady! The wedding is at five [pause for laughter]!" Then he committed [pause] the unpardonable sin [pause]. He called her [pause] the 'B' word [pause] and the silence was deafening [pause].

In this passage, Ed built the tension to a crescendo by steadily increasing the duration of his pauses. His silence spanned the following durations: one second after "then he committed," two seconds after "the unpardonable sin," three seconds after "he called her," four seconds after "the B word," and a full six seconds after "and the silence was deafening." His change in the tone of his content from positive to negative following the "wedding is at five" humorous pause intensified the effect.

Tip #35: Add vocal variety by varying your speed, volume, and pitch

Rory Vaden, who took second place in the 2007 contest, is a man many Toastmasters love to hate. There is something a little too polished about him. Maybe it is his tendency to hold a manufactured smile when he gets laughs. Maybe it is because he has been known to refer to himself as "the 2007 World Champion of Public Speaking [pause] first runner up." And maybe there is a twinge of jealousy, since he has built a successful career through focus and determination as an author and motivational speaker despite not winning the championship.

Love him or hate him, you have to respect Rory's exceptionally deep knowledge of the craft of public speaking. Before he moved from the business of speaking about speaking to the more lucrative market of personal development, he made a major contribution to how Toastmasters think about vocal variety. Though it is impossible to trace its true origin, the grid in Figure 6.1 was popularized by Mr. Vaden.

During inspirational speeches such as those given in the Toastmasters World Championship, speakers spend much of their time in the passionate quadrant with delivery that is loud and relatively snappy. They maintain their volume but slow down to convey major points.

At transitions, speakers typically move to the calming quadrant. It is a zone subconsciously associated with trust building and is often exploited by salespeople just before they close a deal. Many speakers never venture into the suspenseful quadrant. Those who do use it typically reserve it for portions of stories that have a high degree of anxiety or expectation.

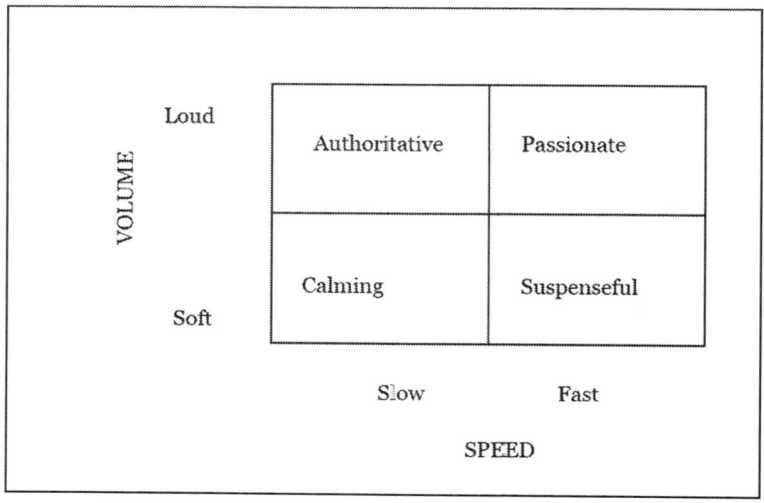

Figure 6.1: Primary dimensions of vocal variety

Since human beings are conditioned to detect change, the key to holding audience interest is to use contrast. If you naturally speak soft and slow, then you can emphasize points by moving to the loud and fast quadrant, the opposite extreme. The converse is also true; passionate speakers can highlight messages by moving to a more calming delivery.

There is no "optimal" quadrant. Any will do as your primary vocal zone. However, you must be careful not to stay in one quadrant too long. If your delivery is unrelentingly passionate, you will overwhelm your audience. They are likely to judge you a zealot and emotionally disconnect. If your delivery is constantly calming, then you will soothe them into boredom. Again, contrast is the key.

The four combinations of volume and speech can be applied to phrases, sentences, and longer passages. However, they can also be applied to individual words. In particular, engaging speakers strive to punch up descriptive adjectives and adverbs with passionate delivery. This is a way to make your energy and enthusiasm infectious. The underlined words and phrases in the passage below from Palaniappa's speech indicate where he boosted the energy level by increasing volume and speed:

In 2004, I had <u>just</u> saved up enough money to buy my first property. I went around scouting for all the properties in the city center, and I found one that I <u>really</u> liked. The <u>price</u>... just over a million dollars. <u>Way out of my budget</u>. The <u>frustration</u> was there, and you know whenever we are frustrated, we try to take it out on someone. Always the victims are those who are nearest and dearest. Since I was not married back then, it was my father.

I like to refer to volume and speed as the primary dimensions of vocal variety since they are the easiest for speakers to consciously manipulate. However, I use the words "consciously manipulate" with some trepidation. The reason for that is because authenticity is the most important characteristic of great public speaking. And authenticity does not take effort. It simply requires you to speak as you would to someone that you care about.

That is easy to do when you are comfortable. But standing in front of tens, hundreds, or especially thousands of people, causes many presenters to speak in a way that is disconnected from the emotional content of the actual words they are saying. They become somewhat muted and robotic. The best way out is to amplify the variety of your natural delivery until you restore your natural manner of speaking.

After volume and speed, pitch is the next most frequently tuned aspect of vocal variety. With individual words, pitch varies from low to high. In addition, speakers can convey curiosity by gradually increasing pitch to form an upward inflexion at the end of a sentence. Note that too many upward inflexions will come across as youthful and lacking confidence. Downward inflexion, created by lowering the pitch at the end of a sentence, conveys decisiveness and poise.

There are more subtle dimensions of vocal variety, including: rhythm, also referred to as cadence or melody, which ranges from monotone to dynamic; quality, ranging from breathy to full; and enunciation, ranging from gentle to crisp. Thinking too hard about these levers, though, is mostly counterproductive to effective public speaking. Instead, match the emotional tone (happy, sad, angry, excited, etc.) of a given part of your speech with your delivery. Then, crank it up a notch or two—or three with a very large audience—to compensate for the effect of nervousness on your voice.

Tip #36: Eliminate all filler words

Anyone who has ever tried to eliminate his or her filler words knows that the process is a lot like trying to fix an old, leaky dam. You eliminate one and another one comes pouring out somewhere else. As discussed previously, pausing for one beat at commas and two beats at periods will eliminate the most common fillers including "um," "ah," "like," and "you know."

Being judged at multiple levels ensures that only people who have learned to eliminate those jarring filler words make it to the final round. However, three new words often appear in the speech patterns of even expert speakers. In particular, speakers who have rooted out other fillers begin starting too many of their sentences with "so," "and," and "but." Even when the usage is grammatically correct, using too many of these words will cause an audience to either consciously or subconsciously view a speaker as less polished. Contest judges are on the lookout particularly for these filler words, since there is often so little separating one finalist from another.

Unfortunately for Palaniappa, he had not yet learned to control for these additional filler words. He started five sentences with "but," six with "so," and ten with "and."

Palaniappa, like most speakers, was likely completely unaware of his tendency to use these three fillers. And, unfortunately, the pausing technique does not cure them. But, there is a cure.

To eliminate filler words at the beginning of sentences, you should do two things. First, detect the problem. The best way to do that is by watching a video recording of one of your speeches. Second, if you have the problem, you need to find a friend willing to watch you give a speech a few times. Have your friend make a noise; for example, tap a pen on the table every time you use "so," "and," or "but." It should take only two or three separate sessions until you are cured.

Tip #37: Use audience participation to keep listeners engaged

Even during a short five-to-seven-minute speech, it is challenging to grab and hold the audience's attention. Since most, but not all, audience participation is verbal, this is a fitting place to understand whether such involvement is a good thing or a bad one.

The first speaker of the day to use audience participation, Stuart Pink, did so two times. In the first instance, he asked the audience members for verbal confirmation that they wanted to hear the secret to creative thinking:

How can you become a brain lifter? Why not use the two most important words in the English language. Without these two tiny words, our world would not exist. Do you want to hear what they are? Say yes. [Audience: Yes!] 'What if?'

In the second instance, Stuart used a far more common type of audience participation known as call-and-response. As revealed in the following passage, he had his audience actually finish his speech:

So, next time you have a problem, do some brain lifting. Next time you face a challenge, ask yourself, what if? Next time you have a dream, ask yourself, what if? No matter what obstacles you face, there is no wrong place. There is no wrong time to ask... [Audience: 'What if?']

Having your audience deliver the final words, words the speaker used repetitively, is a technique adopted by three of the seventeen winners from 1995 to 2011. In 1996, Willie Jones asked the audience to make the "boing" sound a computer makes after it reboots to let the user know that all systems are operational. In 2000, Ed Tate began his last line with, "It was going to be..." and his audience completed the sentence with, "... one of those days." Ed also did this previously during the body of his speech. Finally, in 2005, Lance Miller repeated Mr. Jones's sound technique when the audience knew to complete "Cha.." with "...ching"—the sound representing validating others with genuine appreciation.

Note that Ed Tate's approach to call-and-response was far less risky than Stuart Pink's. Both drew audience participation two times. In Stuart's case, he used two different calls that required two different responses. Ed's was much tighter, and consequently less risky, since he used the same approach both times. Stated another way, he cleverly combined a call-and-response with a callback.

Again, Stuart was not the only speaker in the 2012 contest to use audience participation. Diane Parker got her audience to sing a matching, alternating call-and-response of "hey, hey, hey, hey."

Though a magic trick is nonverbal, Ronald E. Melvin used it to involve his audience in his storytelling. Palaniappa Subramaniam had the audience members take their shoes off. And finally, Brian Corey encouraged his audience to clap to his beat during his introduction and conclusion.

In most environments, audience participation in one form or another is a valuable way to keep people engaged. It is a bit more risky to do in competitive speaking and should be tested in low-stakes rehearsals.

Tip #38: Sing if it suits you

Though Palaniappa did not sing, five of the nine contestants in the 2012 contest chose to do so. The songs they chose ranged from religious spirituals and rap lyrics to the music made by a pink Fisher-Price musical toilet. Yes, you read that last part right.

It is hard to picture anyone singing or dancing in a normal speaking environment. That is especially true in professional environments. However, in the Toastmasters International Speech

Contest, and in keynote settings, speakers often do sing. By way of reference, five of the seventeen past world champions between 1995 and 2011 sang to a lesser or a greater extent. Two had fantastic voices—Mark Brown and LaShunda Rundles. Two had passable singing talent, including Craig Valentine and Dwayne Smith. One, Randy Harvey, sang the chorus of Simon and Garfunkel's "Cecilia" in the creakiest of voices for humorous effect.

The best conclusion to draw from this is simply to sing if it suits you. It is better if you have great pipes, but fine if you do not.

Finding The Right Shoes

Central message(s)	Contentment
Duration	6.8 Minutes
Words per minute	127
Laughs per minute	1.47

Table 6.2: Vital statistics for *Finding The Right Shoes* by Palaniappa Subramaniam

(Introduction)

Mahatma Gandhi once said, "If all enemies were to step into the shoes of their adversaries, all of the misunderstandings and misadventures in the world would be solved." So I decided to step into my wife's high heeled shoes, and the only thing I understood was the pain.

Contest Chair, fellow judges, ladies and gentlemen. Shoes. They come in many shapes, many sizes. Some are designed to run, some are designed to walk. But at the end of the day, what is their sole purpose? Not this sole.

It is to carry you to your destination in life. Therefore, finding the right shoe should not be a trivial pursuit. When I got up this morning, I couldn't decide. I read the dress code, it said semiformal. So, I came prepared.

But the important question is, why do we often feel that another man's shoes are so much more easier *[sic]* to walk in, and we always want to be in his shoes? And we lose focus on our own shoe that is already here.

(Part 1)

When I was ten years old, I had a very good friend by the name of Andrew. Now, he was living my dream. His father was rich. He had everything he wanted. The best toys, the best games, and he could go to Disneyland Orlando without competing in a speech contest. And every day when school was over, his father would wait in a bright, shiny BMW to pick him up. And there I was waiting, waiting, waiting for my dad to pick me up.

And just recently, Andrew was featured in the news. It doesn't get any better, rubbing salt in the wound. It read, 'Father and son, convicted for drug trafficking.' Suddenly, Andrew's shoes were not so interesting. Suddenly, all of the waiting for my father at school didn't seem so long. We are so fixated on what everything could be that we lose focus on what it is.

(Part 2)

In 2004, I had just saved up enough money to buy my first property. I went around scouting for all the properties in the city center, and I found one that I really liked. The price, just over a million dollars. Way out of my budget. So the frustration was there, and you know whenever we are frustrated, we try to take it out on someone. And always the victims are those who are nearest and dearest. Since I was not married back then, it was my father.

So, as we were driving back home, I was telling my dad, "You know pa, back then, properties here were only 50,000 dollars. If only you had bought one, I would have eventually inherited it!" But eventually as days passed, I found one that I liked. It was in a suburban area and it was in my budget. So I signed the papers hurriedly and submitted my mortgage. When the mortgage came back, I fell short fifteen thousand dollars. At that point in time, I had put in all my savings and I had nothing left. What do I do? I was lost, I was confused.

But suddenly I felt the warmth of the overbearing hands that always had my back. It was my father. And he came to me and he said, "Son. I might not have been able to buy you a house in the city, but I can make sure that my grandson is not disappointed with his father." And he handed me a check for twenty-five thousand dollars, and said, "Go and get your home." At that point, his words struck me so hard that I bent my head down in humility.

And as I saw my father's shoes, they were worn out. He has seen so much of rough terrain in life but we never appreciated what he did, because we always wondered what it could be. What I could have. What it should be. I want a rich father-in-law, I want a rich father, I want to write books like John C. Maxwell. Everything is what *I want, I could, I could, I could*, but have you ever realized *what is*?

(Part 3)

There are millions of people out there who can't afford a single pair of shoes. And yet, many of us who have more than twenty pairs, ladies fifty pairs, you are still complaining. So, why not all of you, take off your shoes right now. I don't want to be alone, come on, take them off. I'm serious. Take your shoes off and look at them. Put them in front of you right now and look at your shoes. Not at me, at your shoes.

And tell yourself that these shoes are designed for me. Tell yourself that no matter what my role is at home, at work or in Toastmasters, no one can fit into these shoes better than me. Appreciate how far these shoes have carried you in life. Appreciate the people who put you in those shoes.

(Conclusion)

At times, we always think it's about finding the right shoes. But in actual fact, it's about fitting into the shoes that are destined for you.

Have you ever thought about that? My shoes, they fit me just right. I have no regrets. Now, I ask you. Do your shoes fit right, or do you still want to trade?

CHAPTER 7:
Nonverbal Delivery

Tip #39: Dress for success

"Our seventh contestant is Kenny Ray Morgan. Afraid of the Dog. Afraid of the Dog. Kenny Ray Morgan." After contest master George Yen shakes Kenny Ray's hand, the first thing that strikes you is how Kenny Ray was dressed. He was dressed to the nines. He was not just wearing any old suit as is the custom for most male competitors; he was wearing a light-grey three-piece herringbone suit. A tasteful fuchsia silk pocket square peeked out from his three-button jacket. Then came the accessories: a fun grey-and-white polka-dot tie, gold cufflinks on his pressed white custom shirt, a lapel pin, a square gold watch, and rings on his left pinky and right index finger. Completing his ensemble were black-and-white wingtip spectator shoes that were all the rage in the 1920s. This was a man oozing style and his delivery was as charismatic as his attire.

One of the unspoken rules of public speaking is to dress slightly better than your audience. If you wear jeans at a black-tie event, then it may be taken as a sign of disrespect. Similarly, if you wear a tuxedo at a casual event, then you appear arrogant.

As the Toastmasters World Championship is a semiformal event, Kenny Ray Morgan was dressed at the upper bound of acceptable.

Since Kenny Ray was physically very active on stage, he might have considered shedding some of his accessories. However, he was fortunate that nothing went flying unintentionally or got in the way. Most speakers should shed all encumbrances before taking the stage, including event badges, phones, and keys. Women should avoid wearing jewelry that makes enough noise to get picked up by a microphone, such as certain necklaces, bracelets, or earrings.

Tip #40: The context determines the costume

The exception to all these restrictions is when a speaker wears a costume on stage. Purists feel that the Toastmasters World Championship should be treated as a speaking contest, orator against orator, rather than as a performance. However, that has not stopped the recent trend toward theatricality.

During the 2012 finals, none of the contestants wore costumes. However, a variety has been worn in past years. The most memorable was the outfit selected by David Henderson. Another world champion, Mark Brown, described his reaction to David's costume: "Back in 2010, David Henderson decked himself out as a fighter pilot, complete with bomber jacket, goggles, and scarf. He reenacted his childhood and brought a very powerful message about love. He stood out with his costume, his presentation style, and had a really, really powerful message."

Because wearing a costume is out of the ordinary, I asked David if he felt this was a risky choice. He shared that he eliminated the risk by wearing a costume for another speech in earlier rounds. During those earlier rounds, he devised a rule, which states that the context comes before the costume. Specifically, David was able to wear a costume because he was sharing a story about childhood, complete with a Halloween costume competition. In that context, the costume was not over the top.

Tip #41: Gesture naturally and frequently to reinforce your words

Amongst all of the contestants, Kenny Ray Morgan used the most expressive hand gestures. Here is what he did with his hands at the beginning of his speech:

(hands down at sides) Mark Twain once said (raises hands symmetrically making counterclockwise circle with left hand and clockwise circle with right), "Do that which you fear most and the death of fear is certain."

(Hands down at sides) Mr. Toastmaster (gestures with left arm, palm up to contest master), fellow Toastmasters (repeats prior gesture but with right arm), guests (hands down at sides), and most vigilant judges. (hands together at chest level then expands symmetrically outward) It was a beautiful summer day (hands down at sides), so I decided I would go and pay my friend a visit. As I approached the fence to his house, (raises both

arms with elbows at ninety degrees) which stood way back up on the hill, (right arm down, gestures with left) I noticed that the dog which was usually locked up in his kennel (gestures in circular motion with finger pointed to outline kennel), was sitting proudly in the front yard (elbows bent and wrists limp as if a dog's paws).

(arms out palms up) Now this dog knew of me, (arms up palms down) but he didn't really know me. (hands down at sides) So I decided to proceed cautiously through the gate (gestures with right arm to open the invisible gate), taking care not to make direct eye contact (left arm down, points to eyes with two fingers of right hand). However, this was a sheep dog. (hands down at sides) As you know, a sheep dog's hair completely covers its face (hands covering his face). (hands down at sides) Well, somehow I must have made eye contact because its ears begin to perk up (hands at ear level, fingers together to pantomime dog's ears), and its hind quarters begin to slowly rise like a cat's hump (arms level with ground, bent at elbows with hand touching at chest level), ready to defend its turf.

The first thing to notice about what Kenny Ray does with his hands is actually what he does with them when he is not gesturing. His "base position" is with his arms comfortably down at his sides with his elbows loose. This is the same base position as all eight of his competitors that day. It is also the same base position as sixteen out of the seventeen prior champions.

The one exception was David Henderson, whose base position was the open steeple—hands symmetrically separated at navel level with elbows bent. The open steeple is the sister gesture to the closed steeple, which is the same concept but with the hands gently touching instead of separated. Steeple gestures are considered to be more formal. Though appropriate in settings when a speaker needs to project authority, steeple gestures are not ideal for the Toastmasters contest, where a more conversational style serves to build deeper emotional connection.

The second thing to notice about Kenny Ray Morgan's gestures is their frequency and variety. Now, you might think that he scripted out his gestures. However, speakers rarely do this. For one thing, it is simply too complicated to remember. But, more importantly, scripted gestures quickly become inauthentic.

When you first start in your public speaking journey, the advice to "gesture naturally" does not seem helpful. But, with time and fewer nerves, your brain will naturally synchronize your gestures to your words and allow you to increase the frequency of gestures as you would in normal conversation. In every day conversation, you will have a mixture of symmetrical and asymmetrical gestures without even thinking about it. Practice will get you to the place where you do not think about your hands, you just use them.

One important consideration is that your gestures should occupy a larger volume of space as the size of the audience grows larger. While learning to use hand gestures in public speaking, strive to gesture above the waist and below the neck. As you gain experience as a speaker, you can expand your gesturing to the full 360- degree sphere that surrounds you.

The final observation with regards to gestures is that Kenny Ray employed rather literal pantomime. He drew out the dog's kennel, he recreated the hair covering the dog's eyes, and he even acted out an angry cat defending its turf. These were not just hand gestures; they were whole body gestures that contributed to a performance. If your style is more reserved oratory, then there is no need to go to this overly demonstrative extreme. However, if you are naturally theatrical, then do as Kenny Ray did and go all the way. In the history of the World Championship, people have had an equal chance of winning with both styles.

Tip #42: Maintain three seconds of eye contact with individuals in a random pattern

After taking center stage at the beginning of his speech, Kenny Ray Morgan began with a three-second dramatic pause. However, rather than single out individuals or sections in the audience as is best practice, he used the time to scan the audience from his left to his right. Throughout his speech, he continued to scan or to jump frenetically, holding eye contact at most for one second at a time.

If you compare Kenny Ray with the 2011 World Champion, Jock Elliott, you will see what highly engaging eye contact looks like. Jock holds eye contact until he reaches the end of a phrase or a sentence. He synchronizes his shifts in eye contact with his comprehension pauses. In practical terms, this means that he holds eye contact with an individual or a section in the audience for roughly three seconds. He maintains the lock even if he is moving on stage.

The reason Jock's eye contact was so much more effective than Kenny Ray's is that longer eye contact builds an emotional bond. Rather than thinking of your audience as a group, think of it as a series of people that you are having individual conversations with in random order. You want everyone to feel as though you have spoken to them with roughly equal frequency, even if it is just once. When you speak to someone, you square your body and head toward them, make eye contact for a few moments, then break, then repeat. Importantly, you are making eye contact, not "eyes contact." If you look a person in one eye, you peer into his or her soul. If you try to look a person in both eyes at the same time, then it will feel to the person like you are looking through him or her.

When you watch people in one-on-one conversations, you notice that the more people trust each other, the lower the amount of interpersonal space between them. This same principle applies on stage as well. When Jock Elliott switches his gaze to a new person, he often moves toward that person. In many cases, he walks right up to the edge of the stage to get as close as possible.

Tip #43: Match your facial expressions to the mood of your content at each moment of your speech

What Kenny Ray lacked in eye contact, he made up for with facial expressiveness.

Most speakers go through a three-step journey on the way to mastering facial expressions. In the first phase, their nerves get the better of them and they remain expressionless no matter what they are saying.

At some point, they get feedback that they look nervous and should smile more. That advice initiates phase two, when speakers smile continually even though the smile may not match the context of their words.

Ultimately, speakers reach the third and final phase. In this phase, speakers match their facial expressions to the emotional mood of their content at each moment of their speech. Kenny Ray was a master of phase three. When he spoke about going to visit his friend, he exuded a warm smile of happiness. When enacting a dog sitting proudly, he tilted his head up and relaxed his facial muscles. At different points in his speech, even if you turned the sound off, you could see him clearly express anger, surprise, fear, pain, confusion, and elation.

The same advice that applies to hand gestures applies to facial expressiveness. Be natural. There is no need to script facial expressiveness. There is no need to think about how you manipulate your occipitofrontalis, buccinator, or platysma. Simply ask yourself if your facial expression matches the tone of your content. Everyone knows how to make a happy face or a sad face and the less you think about it the more genuine the facial expression will be. And, just as with hand gestures, amplify your facial expressiveness as your audience grows larger.

Tip #44: Imbue props with deeper meaning and hide them when not in use

Props were a relative rarity in the Toastmasters International Speech Contest until the year 2000, when Ed Tate used a police speeding-ticket book and an airline ticket. From that year through 2011, seven of the twelve winners used a prop of one type or another.

In Ed's case, he used the prop quite literally. This was also true of David Henderson's aviator costume, complete with hat, bomber jacket, goggles, and scarf. In both cases, the speakers followed the best practice—hiding the props when not in use.

But literal uses of props are less powerful than metaphorical ones. During the 2012 contest, Palaniappa Subramaniam used his own mismatched shoes to convey deeper meaning. His shoes represented the misguided belief that our lives would be better if we could only be somebody else. He took his shoes off at the beginning of his speech then put them back on again at the end.

Past champions have also found clever ways to imbue props with meaning. The 2007 winner, Vikas Ghingran, referred to an envelope containing a graduate-school letter and said, "The answer is inside." Of course, this was a metaphor for the idea that the answers to life's great questions are to be found only inside of ourselves. Similarly, Lance Miller used a parking-garage ticket that needed to be validated as a reminder that we should actively show our appreciation of others.

Though now completely overdone and downright silly to non-Toastmasters, three world champions used chairs as props, including Jim Key in 2003, Randy Harvey in 2004, and LaShunda Rundles in 2008.

Among the three, Randy's was the cleverest by far, since he used a chair to convey multiple meanings. At the beginning of his speech, the chair represented his father's new car—a 1960 Ford Fairlane. Randy, reliving a childhood experience, stood on the chair as a proxy for the roof of the car in order to avoid a pack of hunting dogs that were chasing him.

Later, he transformed the car into his new 1963 Volkswagon Beetle, which he proceeded to crash through a fence and into a neighbor's fountain. During that same vignette, he changed the chair into a rock near the fountain he sat on as his dad comforted him. The speaker, portraying his father, got on bended knee beside the chair, put his arm on the top, and said: "Shhhhh. We can fix the fence. I'll buy another fountain. We can even replace that old car. Those are just things. But, I can never replace you."

Finally, at the end of his speech, Randy turned the speech into his parents' sofa. He caressed the top of the chair when he said, "Their hands always seemed to find each other." Morphing the sofa into his mother, with his arms encircling the chair lovingly from behind, he continued:

And when Momma was sitting and watching TV, Fat Dad would come up behind her, wrap his strong arms around her, rest his chin on her shoulder, and kiss her on the cheek.

Through the course of his speech, Randy transformed the chair into two cars, a rock, the speaker himself, a sofa, and his mother. Randy and his fellow champions have proven that it is reasonably safe to use props in competitive speaking. Just strive to use them creatively and imbue them with deeper meaning.

Tip #45: Move within the virtual set you create on stage

In the same way that contestants use tangible props to make meaning, great speakers bring the intangible to life on the stage. In order to relive your story, you need to create a virtual theatrical set, complete with objects and people.

During his speech, Kenny Ray Morgan shared three vignettes with the following physical elements:

- Outside his friend's house: a dog kennel, a fence with a gate, and a sheepdog
- In a vacant lot: another dog
- On a street on the way home from school: a dog with no teeth and a brick

Kenny Ray demonstrated several best practices. The first involves moving for dramatic effect, known in theater as blocking.

He shared his first vignette, about being chased by his friend's sheepdog, at stage right (the audience's left). He then recreated the vacant lot at center stage. Last, he shared the time another friend was chased by a dog with no teeth at stage left (the audience's right). Western audiences read from left to right and therefore subconsciously expect that chronological stories will be presented that way as well.

Within each of the three minisets, Kenny Ray worked to ensure that objects and people had consistent locations on stage. For example, he described the fence in his first vignette and referenced it with a hand gesture as being in a particular place. Later, he came back to that same spot to open the gate and then to jump over the fence. For the duration of his story, that location on the stage was indelibly burned into the audience's minds as the fence. To that end, Kenny Ray took caution to step over it carefully whenever he came to the spot again.

Kenny Ray Morgan, like other seasoned speakers, also took full advantage of both the width and the depth of the stage. His story world existed mainly in the middle of the stage. That allowed him to come out of the story periodically and engage the audience directly in conversation by moving forward. Some additional tricks of the trade that prior world champions have used include walking the full diagonal of the stage to represent a long journey and moving backward on the stage to go back in time.

Afraid Of The Dog

Central message(s)	Action
Duration	6.9 minutes
Words per minute	123
Laughs per minute	1.73

Table 7.1: Vital statistics for *Afraid Of The Dog* by Kenny Ray Morgan

(Introduction)

Mark Twain once said, "Do that which you fear most and the death of fear is certain."

(Part 1)

Mr. Toastmaster, fellow Toastmasters, guests, and most vigilant judges. It was a beautiful summer day, so I decided I would go and pay my friend a visit. As I approached the fence to his house, which stood way back up on the hill, I noticed that the dog which was usually locked up in his kennel, was sitting proudly in the front yard.

Now this dog knew *of* me, but he didn't really know me. So I decided to proceed cautiously through the gate, taking care not to make direct eye contact. However, this was a sheep dog. As you know, a sheep dog's hair completely covers its face. Well, somehow I must have made eye contact because its ears begin to perk up, and its hind quarters begin to slowly rise like a cat's hump, ready to defend its turf.

It started to growl and make that hyperventilating sound. You know the one—Grrr, hee. Grrr, hee. Uh oh! At this point, I didn't need a genius to tell me I was in serious trouble. I broke out into an all-out sprint for that fence, all the while running angrily, thinking 'Who let the dog out? Who? Who? Who let the dog out? Who, who?' As I approached that fence, it was my idea to do a leap and over. Pretty good idea, huh? Except the dog must have been thinking the same thing.

When I leaped clear of that fence, it leaped too. The next thing I felt was his sharp teeth penetrating deep into my right buttocks. Ladies and gentlemen, have you ever had an animal sink its teeth deep into your flesh? If not, trust me, a nurse's booster shot would have been a welcome treat in comparison. Screaming in pain, I fought frantically to remove that dog's jaws from my flesh. I even pleaded with him, 'Please, release me. Let me go.'

Finally, after making it over that fence, I vowed never to go to that house again. They lost a very good friend that day. However, this would not be my last encounter with a canine.

(Part 2)

Just five years later, while crossing a big vacant lot, I spotted a huge barking dog. I had instant flashbacks of that first fateful encounter, and I started to run.

While running, a small, still voice asked a question, 'How long are you going to be afraid?' At that moment, I stopped, and decided I wouldn't be afraid anymore. I turned directly towards that dog and I start running at him and screaming at him and hollering at him. The dog stopped dead in its tracks, looking curious, as if to think, 'What manner of man is this that he would come chasing after a ferocious, barking dog?'

With me continuing toward him like a crazed fool, he decided not to stick around to find out. He tucked his tail and ran away as fast as he could.

I learned a very valuable lesson that day. If we insist on running away from our fears, they will continue to chase and harass us, gaining strength in the process. But when we take courage and face our fears, their powers will soon diminish and they'll lose their grip on our lives.

(Part 3)

There's no need to be afraid of the dog. As the old African proverb says, "If there's no enemy within, the enemy on the outside can do us no harm."

This saying would serve me well, when I had my friend give me a related situation concerning another stray neighborhood dog. He would recall how this dog would bark and chase him every day after school. Until finally, one day, he declared if this dog comes after me one more time, I'm going to teach it a lesson.

Sure enough, one day while walking home, minding his own business, this dog came out of nowhere, chasing and running him down. Frantically, while running scared out of his wits, he stopped, picked up a brick, turned to face the dog which was right up on him, only to discover that the dog didn't have any teeth. He threw the brick down, told the dog, 'Get on out of my way.'

(Conclusion)

Ladies and gentlemen, what are you running from today? Is the fear of the dog in your life keeping you from realizing your greatest potential? So many of us go through life running scared; running from things that have no teeth and can do us no harm. They have more bark than bite. So, we should act with urgency when dealing with our fears. After all, we don't have forever. As the old saying goes, 'Life is like a roll of toilet tissue. The closer we get to the end, the faster it runs out.'

Let's embrace our fears, thus making them our allies that motivate us, rather than our foes that stifle us. It's no wonder why Helen Hayes, the stage actress, once said, "Fear is a familiar friend, a constant companion. Always nagging me to do my best."

Ladies and gentlemen, there's no need to be afraid of the dog. We should all heed the wise words of one Mark Twain, when he says, "Do that which you fear most, and the death of fear is certain." Mister Toastmaster.

Chapter 8:
Mind-set

Tip #46: Train like a champion

"Our eighth speaker is Ryan Avery. Trust is a Must. Trust is a Must. Ryan Avery."

When I began doing research for this book, the first thing I did was to reach out to the 2012 finalists and to as many past champions as possible. The first person to take my call was the 2012 contestant, Ryan Avery. I asked Ryan and all of the others the same question: "What are your best pieces of advice on how to win the World Championship of Public Speaking?"

On some level, I was hoping to discover that the winners had certain tactical advice on content development, verbal delivery, and nonverbal delivery that the losers did not have. However, win or lose, they all had more or less the same set of advice. In his own words, here is the mind-set that Ryan carried before he stepped onto the stage:

The first thing I tell everyone is to practice how you play. If you think like a champion and train like a champion, then you will be a champion. I woke up every day at 5:00 a.m. and practiced for two uninterrupted hours. Over the course of a year, the difference between my waking up at 5 a.m. and you waking up at 7 a.m. is 31 extra days—the equivalent of an extra month.

I practiced, I practiced, I practiced at every single opportunity that I could. I spoke countless times in my (Toastmasters) District. Every time I traveled for work, I set up speeches with local clubs. I wouldn't just practice with Toastmasters; I practiced anywhere that made me feel uncomfortable... in the middle of Downtown Pioneer Square Portland, in the gym sauna where people would look at me funny, at jails... even underwater so that I could learn when to pause and come up for a breath because I am a fast speaker.

I practiced my semi-final winning speech 'Push Past It' for five months up through the District Contest. I then switched over to preparing 'Trust is a Must' for the next three months.

I practiced everything including entering and leaving the stage with energy. I even practiced wearing a suit from 5 am to 11 pm because I knew that is what I would be wearing (at the competition) in Florida and needed to know I would be comfortable.

You want to practice to the point where you send the same message no matter how you deliver your speech. My message of "Trust Is A Must" needs to be just as powerful whether you read it, watch it, or listen to it. Practicing by videotaping is essential. Watch yourself. But, more importantly, send it to your mentors for feedback.

You have to tell yourself that you are stronger than your mind. I would catch myself sometimes saying things like 'Hey, if I get 2nd place this year, then that is fine.' But I then thought 'Why is that fine Ryan? You are putting yourself in a position to fail.' A champion does not think she is going to get second place. She thinks she is going to win. When people don't laugh at your speech or when people give you feedback that throws you off, you must go back to the message you want to deliver and how you can connect with your audience and inspire them.

Just before I walk up to deliver a speech, I think about Lady Gaga's song 'Marry The Night' to build my confidence. When I heard that for the first time, it really moved me. She wrote that song in a coffee shop one night when she said 'From this point forward, I am going to marry myself to my music.' That is how I feel about speaking. I am there for the audience and for the message.

You can use a song lyric or you can think about a time when you felt confident. Maybe you got a good grade on a test. Maybe you asked someone out on a date and they said yes. Put that in your mind right before you speak and you will exude confidence.

You have to surround yourself with people that are better than you. I broke people up into certain categories (of expertise). I like you for your humor... I like you for your body language... I like you for your vocal variety. I recorded myself and sent videos out to my League of Extraordinary Mentors and asked for specific advice on areas that they were great at. That helped me build the different chuncks of the speech.

I would have people turn around and listen to me. I would have others watch my video without sound. And, I would have some who would both watch and listen. When all three groups got the same message, I knew I was on the right path. Your mentors are the ones that will help you do that.

Finally, you should have one primary mentor; Randy Harvey (2004 champion) is the Chairman of my speaking Board of Directors. My League of Extraordinary Mentors rounds out my Board with expertise in specific areas.

Tip #47: Deliver the best speech you can

Having trained like a champion, Ryan knew that the only thing left for him to do was to deliver the best speech he could. Doing that means letting go of what the speech and the speech contest means to you and instead focusing on delivering an essential message that changes the lives of your audience. In Ryan's case, that message was "trust is a must."

Ryan used the same flashback narrative pattern that Vikas Ghingran used back in 2007. Ryan started his speech in one moment—his wedding day—and then wound the clock back to three vignettes ultimately returning to the initial scene. Ryan's first vignette revealed the importance of personal honesty in establishing trust. His second exposed the insight that "a promise is only as good as the person who makes it." Finally, the third vignette showed that trust is the basis of love.

Like Ryan, fellow competitor Stuart Pink stressed the importance of focusing on your message to deliver the best speech you can when he shared, "Though it may sound paradoxical, my first piece of advice is don't try to win. Making a connection with the audience is what matters. If you are all about trying to win, then I don't think it is going to happen."

In addition to sharing your most important message with the audience, the current challengers and past winners stress that the competition is critical to your growth as a speaker. The Distinguished Toastmaster (DTM) award is the highest achievement that can be earned by Toastmasters. To earn a DTM, individuals must complete a number of leadership requirements and deliver forty speeches. However, the quality of the speeches has no bearing on the award. A speaker just needs to deliver them. Moreover, every speech is different.

The various speech contests, including the International Speech Contest that is the basis for the World Championship, fill an important gap in the Toastmasters experience. The contest environment forces speakers to refine the content and delivery of a single speech. Though everyday public speaking does not demand that level of preparation, it is a required skill for anyone seeking to build a career as a public speaker.

Tip #48: Make a friend of your public-speaking fear

Someone once asked me, "Does the fear of public speaking ever go away?" The short answer is "no" and anyone that claims otherwise is lying to you. You just learn to make that fear your friend and channel it into your performance. The second contestant of the day, Andrew Kneebone, confirmed this:

"I guess it all begins with the reasons why we all joined Toastmasters. I joined Toastmasters because I realized that wherever I'm going in my career, I will need to speak in public. Fear or no fear, I recognized that without training I most likely would do it badly. During the biggest moments in my life, I am going to have people in front of me—my bosses or my peers. Or, it could be my wedding. Those are the times where you really don't want to stuff it up."

"After twelve months in Toastmasters, I wanted to take it to the next level. I realized that the more that you confront the fears of public speaking in this nurturing environment, the more fear is no longer a stranger. That feeling I get in my chest... he's a friend now. If you know how to harness that energy, then it's going to do some pretty cool things for you. That's why I decided to compete."

Andrew's comments are spot on. The single best way to control fear is through continual practice. Beyond that, here are some additional tips on controlling fear that the 2012 finalists, prior world champions, and others have shared.

Prior to the event:

- Rehearse at least three times per day, preferably with video recording
- Seek feedback from experts
- Visit the site well in advance of the day you are presenting
- Get regular sleep and exercise
- Understand all important logistical considerations, such as the room setup, audience size, and technology

On the day of the event:

- Exercise
- Drink warm decaffeinated liquid and eat a light meal
- Arrive early to familiarize yourself with the environment and make any necessary modifications
- Network with the audience beforehand
- Listen to music to distract and energize you

During your speech:

- Remember that your audience wants you to succeed
- Pause and slow down, since nerves will make you talk fast
- Take slow, deliberate diaphragmatic breaths (expand your stomach when you breathe in and contract your stomach when you breath out; you are doing it right if your shoulders are not moving when you breathe)
- Keep notes in your pocket
- Focus on your audience, not yourself

Tip #49: Get feedback from experts

Included in the fear-reducing tips is the advice to seek feedback from experts. Experienced speakers know that feedback can be as damaging as it is constructive. At its best, great feedback can transform you as a speaker. At its worst, bad feedback can shatter your confidence.

The critical part of processing feedback is separating fact from opinion. When a single person gives you advice, it is worthy of consideration but not yet worthy of action. However, if multiple people give you the same advice, then you should take corrective action in most circumstances.

Everyone is qualified to provide you with feedback on how your speech made them feel. Then, it is up to you to determine what to do with that information. At the beginning of Darren LaCroix's winning speech, he intentionally fell on the floor to illustrate what the fear of failure feels like. When he practiced this in front of other Toastmasters, they said: "Get up sooner, I was uncomfortable." His coach, the 1995 World Champion, Mark Brown, said: "Stay down longer, they are uncomfortable." Mark was right and it was a big part of what helped Darren win. This story illustrates that you must be thoughtful about how and where you seek feedback and what you do with it.

Trust Is A Must

Central message(s)	Trust
Duration	6.75 Minutes
Words per minute	112
Laughs per minute	2.22

Table 8.1: Vital statistics for *Trust Is A Must* by Ryan Avery

(Introduction)

I'm at the altar, sweating in my wool suit. She is glowing in her white dress. Asks me the most important question of my life, 'Ryan, do you promise me?'

(Part 1)

Before I make my commitment, I let my mind rewind like an old-school VHS tape. And it takes me back to high school, when I would plead with my mom to let me go to parties. "Mom, please let me go? There'll be no alcohol, I promise."

Mom in her nightgown and bunny slippers smiled sweetly. "All right. I trust you." Mister contest chair, fellow Toastmasters, anybody who has ever lied to Mama before.

We're having fun in a field in small-town Texas. My friend Taylor passes me another beer when bright lights freeze us in place. The man behind the lights, big belly over a belt buckle, lip full of dip. Sheriff Snodgrass caught us red-handed, red solo cups in hand.

"Boys, it's your lucky night. Either fill this bag to the top with cigarette butts, or we start calling mamas." We grabbed that bag and there we were, three macho teenagers, Taylor, Eric and, well ... two macho teenagers... and me; crawling in a semi sober state collecting soggy cigarette butts all night.

Next morning, we took that bag and we dropped it off at the station. There is some angry southern woman yelling in a night-gown and bunny slippers. Like a human bulldozer, mom plows through the crowd. "Son, what's happened?"

"Mom, if you ever worried about me smoking, don't. The guys and I had to pick up five pounds of cigarette butts."

"Why, Ryan?"

"There was alcohol at the party mom."

"Son, I am disappointed. Worse, I can't believe you. Trust is a must. Times have changed. When dad and I were your age, we picked up seven pounds."

(Part 2)

It took me a long time to earn mom's trust back, and after a sum-mer of her house arrest, it was my senior year and I became a wannabe entrepreneur. This man offered me buckets of money to build him a website. New car, here I come.

I spent weeks hunched in a chair, glued to a screen, typing on a Cheetos-stained keyboard. I finished, we met, handed over the files. He checked for his checkbook, couldn't find it. Promised he would send a check over immediately. No problem. We shook hands, I'll get paid in a couple of days.

Well, a couple of days passed and where I'm from, handshakes mean something. I called him. His phone is disconnected. I googled him. He gave me a fake name. What? I complained to mom, and do you know what she said? "Trust is a must, isn't it son?"

Don't you hate when parents are right. Like one of those annoying hotel alarm clocks, it woke me up. How was I supposed to expect a man to keep a handshake, when I couldn't even keep a promise to mom? I learned a promise is only as good as the person who makes it.

(Part 3)

I was finally able to leave small-town Texas and I went to college in Colorado, and I met the girl. Tall, curly hair, a tattoo or two.

She is beautiful, and I'm just some punk with pimples. After a few hours of laughing she is bringing-home-to-mama material. A couple of dates later, I was upfront. I said, "Chelsea, I'm not looking for a girlfriend, I'm looking for a wife. I'm leaving the country, won't be back for seven months and I want kids. Warning though, this, twelve pounds at birth."

Sorry mom. I have no idea how I convinced that girl to be my girlfriend, but I did. We started building our foundation of trust three thousand miles apart. I wrote her a hand-written letter every day while I was gone. I doodled what our kids would look like. Dreamed of still holding her hand at ninety. Decided no bunny slippers.

When I got back home, I met with Chelsea's parents, and I got that seal of approval. I told them, "One day I'll have more business experience. I'll do my best raising a couple of twelve-pound babies. I will love that girl when her curls turn grey."

(Conclusion)

Before the wedding, my mom reminded me that trust is a must if I want this marriage to last.

I am at the altar, sweating in my wool suit, and Chelsea is glowing in her white dress. "Chelsea, I promise."

CHAPTER 9:
Leaving the Stage

Tip #50: Pause to let your final words sink in before yielding the stage

"Our ninth and final speaker is Mario Lewis. Don't Look. Don't Look. Mario Lewis."

Among the first tips covered in this book, one is to take the stage with confidence. Mario Lewis not only walked out with confidence, he muttered to himself under the veil of applause "I'm going to have some fun today." It was quiet enough to be missed by the audience and judges, but loud enough to be picked up on the replay.

True to his personal promise, he looked like he had a great time sharing his story and his message about the power of positivity. He got his first laugh before he even finished his first sentence by starting with, "I was relaxing on the couch, watching the New York Nicks beat the Orlando Magic..." This joke was custom-tailored for the audience, since the contest was held in Orlando, Florida. Over the course of his speech, he captured fourteen more laughs. By averaging 2.1 laughs per minute, he claimed the imaginary prize for third-funniest speaker.

At various points in his story, Mario lost his job and his home. In his darkest hour, his thirteen-month-old daughter was diagnosed with juvenile diabetes. And, in that moment, Mario's mentor, his mother-in-law, rode in with the message of positive perspective, "Be thankful. You are so blessed to still have your baby girl."

He delivered his final words, "Don't look (*two-second pause*), live on the brighter side (*four-second pause*). Mr. Contest Chair." Holding that four-second pause at the end of his speech took tremendous restraint, especially after delivering an emotionally powerful speech with a passionate conclusion.

Tip #51: Exit confidently

In the Toastmasters International Speech Contest and in every other environment, speakers are judged from the moment they enter until the moment they leave (or sit down). After saying "Mr. Contest Chair," he gestured in appreciation to John Lau. As applause erupted, Mario stood in silent gratitude with a gentle smile for another three seconds. Holding his smile, he walked off with his head held high.

Nearly every other 2012 contestant ended his or her speech in the same way—with a gesture toward the contest master and then a confident walk off the stage. But, there were a couple of differences that are worth looking into.

One difference was that the first contestant, Andrew Kneebone, shook the hand of the contest master prior to leaving the stage. Ten of the seventeen prior World Champions shook the hand of the contest master. When not otherwise prohibited by the contest rules, I advise shaking the contest master's hand as a sign of respect. This is something that speakers in almost every other environment are accustomed to doing as a way to turn the stage back to the emcee.

The second difference was that two contestants, Palaniappa Subramaniam and Ryan Avery, waved to the audience as they left the stage. This is a practice used by five of the past seventeen world champions. This too is worth doing as a sign of comfort and of appreciation for your audience. In the same category are bows or curtsies. Though no one did so in the 2012 contest, seven of the past seventeen world champions did and it is a good idea for the same reasons as waving.

This brings us to the third and final difference. Ryan Avery did not just walk off the stage as he waved; he jogged off waving, and at a pretty healthy trot. Only one prior champion, Randy Harvey in 2004, did this. In fact, with the exception of shaking the contest master's hand (Randy did and Ryan did not), their exit was identical. Since Randy was Ryan's coach, this is a good sign that Randy's coaching covered every aspect of the world championship. Now, if everyone jogged, then it would become cliché.

However, being the only one to do it in a contest demonstrates a highly energetic, memorable departure.

The final consideration in leaving the stage is to be confident but not too confident. Even in a speech contest, your mission has more to do with inspiring your audience than it has to do with winning. During the 2012 contest, all of the competitors exhibited great poise leaving the stage and maintained their emotional bond with the audience. That characterization also applies to all of the prior champions, with two notable exceptions. In 1999, Craig Valentine pumped his left fist. In 2001, Darren LaCroix did a double fist pump. At that moment, both speakers were in their own heads and signaling, "Yeah, I nailed it." To be sure, they both did, giving two of the strongest speeches ever to grace the stage of the World Championship. However, those fist pumps could very well have turned off judges and cost them their contests. It is best to save the celebration for private moments after you leave the stage.

Don't Look

Central message(s)	Positivity
Duration	6.8 Minutes
Words per minute	115
Laughs per minute	2.06

Table 9.1: Vital statistics for *Don't Look* by Mario Lewis

(Introduction)

I was relaxing on the couch, watching the New York Nicks beat the Orlando Magic, when my very pregnant wife says, "We need to talk." Which means she will be doing all of the talking. "To help us with the new baby, my mother has agreed to move in with us."

"Agreed? I didn't know we had asked," is what I said to myself. I knew better than to argue with my pregnant wife.

Mr. Contest Chair, friends. When my mother-in-law moved in, I got tons of advice. I was told to look on the brighter side. Why? Instead of *looking*, why don't we *live* on the brighter side? There is a difference. Looking is temporary. We do it every now and then, hoping, waiting for good things to happen. Living is a mindset, that no matter the problems or pitfalls ahead, you will have a positive attitude. You are open to a world of happiness when you live on the brighter side.

(Part 1)

Living on the brighter side is not easy, I know. Back in 2002, within a five-week period, I lost my job, my apartment, and my girlfriend. If I lost a dog and an old pickup truck, I would have had a country music song. I walked around in a cloud of negativity, and I was miserable. I had only myself to blame. I was so consumed with the things I had lost that I turned my back on everything that I had to gain.

(Part 2)

What have you missed by not living with a positive attitude? To get to the brighter side, put aside the pain of your past so that you can focus on your future.

When our daughter, Sydney, was born, the good doctor handed her to me. My first words, "Wow. My little princess. She is so little."

Without missing a beat, my wife, who had just endured hours of painful labor, looked up and said her first words. "Mmm, mmm. She wasn't that small."

Then I handed little Sydney to her. She just melted. Before, she was consumed with the pain she had been through. With Sydney in her arms, she could now focus on the promise and the potential of our future.

(Part 3)

Put aside your pain of your past. Benefit from every situation, even the difficult ones. Nine months after Sydney was born, I lost my job again.

The following morning, I lay in bed, watching my wife get dressed for work. I turned to her and I said, "I guess this makes you my sugar mama, huh?" I could actually joke about the situation. My job loss was an opportunity to spend quality time at home with my daughter. I saw Sydney take her first steps. A precious moment I would have missed by not living on the brighter side.

(Part 4)

Celebrate your small achievements every day. One time, I walked into the bathroom and there was Sydney. Sitting on her pink Fisher-Price musical potty. My mother-in-law looked up, looked me straight in the eye and said, "You agreed to help with the potty training." You can see where my wife gets it from.

Then all of a sudden we heard 'Do, do do do do do.' The potty went off! My mother-in-law started clapping and cheering, little Sydney on her potty started clapping and cheering, and they looked at me. I looked back at them. They looked back at me. I had no choice but to start clapping and cheering. By celebrating your small achievements, you too can get through your stinky situations.

(Part 5)

Have faith that the brighter side will come, because there will be times when your faith will be tested. At thirteen months, our little Sydney became suddenly ill. She was diagnosed with juvenile diabetes.

I was heartbroken. It was there in the recovery room where my mother-in-law, a woman of great faith, noticed the toll that it was taking on me. As the tears welled in my eyes, she gave me a warm embrace and whispered, "Be thankful. You are so blessed to still have your baby girl." Of all the people, she was the one reminding me to live on the brighter side.

Now at three years old, Sydney is happy, she's healthy, and full of life.

(Conclusion)

Ten years ago, I *looked* on the brighter side. My happiness was temporary. Today, I *live* on the brighter side. It's permanent.

Fellow Toastmasters and friends, as you maneuver the ups and downs and twists and turns of this amazing journey we call life, put aside your pain. Benefit from every situation. Celebrate your small achievements. And, always have faith. Don't *look, live* on the brighter side. Mr. Contest Chair.

CHAPTER 10:
And the Winner Is…

Sitting in the audience after Mario Lewis left the stage, I felt completely confused as to who had won the contest. I turned to my two friends flanking me, and they too shrugged their shoulders. With nine amazing speakers, the contest was too close to call. In fact, none of us actually picked the winner on the sample ballots we had been filling in over the course of the contest. Additionally, no speaker was disqualified for going over time.

After deep analysis and hundreds of replays, I began to see each speaker's key strengths and weaknesses relative to the best practices enumerated in this book. Let's look at each speaker:

Andrew Kneebone: Andrew had a strong core message of respect and perseverance. However, his comparatively low amount of humor, visible nervousness, and dual-protagonist narrative structure would likely be a drag on his scores.

Stuart Pink: Stuart had both a novel title, "Brain Lifting," and a unique message about creativity. His storytelling was also strong and, because it involved children, was broadly applicable. The wild card was how the judges would interpret his starting and ending his speech with jumping jacks.

Ronald E. Melvin: Ronald had an extremely well-constructed three-part narrative structure he used to deliver a compelling message that we must turn disaster into laughter. He was also the funniest speaker of the day, with an eye-popping 3.3 laughs per minute. However, the magic trick he did in his introduction was rather disconnected from the rest of his speech. Many audience members and judges were likely left stunned, momentarily trying to figure out how he did the trick.

Brian Corey: Brian told an excellent story with a clear message of perseverance. However, he also delivered the fewest laughs in the contest.

Diane Parker: Diane had the most emotionally powerful speech of the day. So much so, that she left the stage with controlled tears welling in her eyes. When I watched her, I got the sense this was a speech that she felt compelled to deliver. She wanted the audience to join her in forgetting the pain of the past in order to mindfully embrace the promise of the present. However, her speech was overly religious and too dark for a broad audience.

Palaniappa Subramaniam: In addition to his well-constructed story, Palaniappa stood out for the very clever use of his shoes as props imbued with a deeper metaphorical meaning that tied to his core theme. Though he was a master of the pause, his use of "and," "so," and "but" as filler words would put at least a small dent in his armor. In addition, he got slightly tongue-twisted during critical moments in his introduction.

Kenny Ray Morgan: Kenny Ray was the day's strongest performance-driven storyteller. With facial expressions, gestures, and movement, he relived with the audience what it was like to be chased by dogs on three separate occasions. In recent years, Toastmasters judges have rewarded theatrical performance. However, there is growing concern in the broader Toastmasters community that things are getting "over the top" and drifting away from the true oratory valued in the real world. There were only two other small nits to be picked with Kenny Ray's performance. The first was his frenetic eye contact. The second is that he was a bit tongue-twisted in the transition to his third vignette.

Ryan Avery: Ryan's speech was rooted in a message, trust, which was novel. He also had the second-funniest speech and used a flashback narrative pattern that deftly kept the audience members on the edge of their seats. Ryan's performance was as "over the top" as Kenny Ray's. At one point, he was crawling on the floor reenacting a drunken stupor. Since the rest of his speech was flawless, he would win or lose on the basis of whether the judges appreciated his theatrical behavior.

Mario Lewis: With great humor, compelling storytelling, and an inspiring message, Mario was my pick to win the contest. The one consideration that might have held him back was that he packed too much into his speech with an introduction, a five-part body, and a conclusion.

When the dust settled, Stuart Pink took home third place with "Brain Lifting." His jumping jacks held him back a little, but not much. Palaniappa Subramaniam took home second place. The first few times I rewatched his speech, I was deeply puzzled as to why he did not win. On deeper inspection, it was clear that at least some of the judges would have picked up on his filler words and deducted points for his early verbal stumble.

And the winner is... Ryan Avery. At twenty-five years old, Ryan was the youngest winner in the history of the Toastmasters contest. With his focused preparation, novel topic, great humor, and flawless delivery, he more than earned it. If you take theatrical performance out of the equation, he was the undeniable champion.

Acknowledgments

In 1998, I changed jobs from being a semiconductor engineer to a semiconductor analyst. That probably sounds like a small change to most people, but it was a gargantuan leap for me. With that move, I could no longer hide in my cubicle. I would need to learn to speak in public to build my career.

And so it was that I walked into my first Toastmasters meeting during lunch one day in Gartner Inc.'s office in San Jose, California. I took great care to sit in the back of the room. This went on for many meetings, until Joshua Reynolds and Grant Dubois dragged me kicking and screaming to the front of the room to deliver my first table topic. And yes, it was horrific for me and for my audience. Josh and Grant, though our lives have taken us down different paths, thank you for starting my journey as a speaker.

Over the years, I have had the honor of watching many great speakers in Toastmasters clubs around the world. I also got to deliver a few speeches of my own. Thank you to my fellow Toastmasters, past and present, who taught me indirectly by example and directly through constructive feedback. I am especially grateful to the members of my two home clubs—Greater Stamford Toastmasters and Gartner Toastmasters.

Of course, this book would not have been possible without the guidance of the past World Champions and the 2012 contestants. Watching you live and on video, I felt that I got to know you just a little bit. I would like to especially acknowledge the individuals who took time out of their busy daily lives to openly share their wisdom including: Ryan Avery, Stuart Pink, Andrew Kneebone, David Brooks, Mark Brown, Craig Valentine, Ed Tate, Darren LaCroix, Lance Miller, Vikas Jhingran, David Henderson, and Jock Elliott.

Lastly, and most importantly, thank you to my family. Irene, thank you for making me believe that it is still quality time when I'm sitting elbow to elbow with you watching "The Daily Show" and "The Colbert Report" while I—cloaked in noise-cancelling headphones—bang away at my keyboard. To my children, thank you for believing that Daddy is a good writer even if you refuse to read his "impenetrable grown-up books." I couldn't be prouder that you know how to use the word "impenetrable" correctly in a sentence.

19670103R00104

Made in the USA
Charleston, SC
06 June 2013